**INSTRUCTOR'S MANUAL
TO ACCOMPANY**

# *American 24-Karat Gold*

## *24 Classic American Short Stories*

### *Second Edition*

**Yvonne Collioud Sisko**
*Middlesex County College*

PEARSON
Longman

New York   San Francisco   Boston
London   Toronto   Sydney   Tokyo   Singapore   Madrid
Mexico City   Munich   Paris   Cape Town   Hong Kong   Montreal

Senior Acquisitions Editor: Susan Kunchandy
Senior Supplements Editor: Donna Campion
Electronic Page Makeup: Lorraine Patsco

Instructor's Manual to Accompany *American 24-Karat Gold — 24 Classic American Short Stories*, 2/e, by Yvonne Collioud Sisko

Please visit our website at: http://www.ablongman.com

ISBN: 0-321-36563-1

1 2 3 4 5 6 7 8 9 10 - OPM - 08 07 06 05

# TABLE OF CONTENTS
# INSTRUCTOR'S MANUAL

# TO THE INSTRUCTOR

The pedagogical apparatus surrounding each story has been carefully designed to maximize student involvement and simultaneously to provide you with multiple, administratively efficient diagnostic and assessment tools. Each story is set up as an individual lesson and each is aimed at increasing comprehension and at reinforcing and/or applying other classroom reading studies.

For the student, each story starts by applying solving words in context, then solving words by structural attack, then by offering pre-reading, purpose questions—all intended to increase accessibility to the story—and then by offering a brief, biographical blurb on the author. Please note that the context words have been chosen because they are essential to understanding the story, while the structural words have been chosen because they apply this form of attack well. Each story is followed by materials that actively involve the student in the reading. First, the Journal asks the student to think about, to record, and to apply:

- MLA formatting

- main from supporting characters separation (reinforcing separating main ideas from supporting details)

- setting identification (reinforcing making inferences)

- sequence organization (reinforcing sequencing)

- plot summarization (reinforcing summarizing)

- conflict explanation (reinforcing making judgments)

- significant quotations explanation (reinforcing making inferences)

Second, the Follow-up Questions focus the student on comprehension feedback. The student can express her/his understanding in objective, short answer subjective, and/or subjective essay format, at your discretion. Third, Discussion Questions encourage personal and literary debate and can be used for class discussion, for group discussion, and/or for individual writing. Finally, Writing provides prompts for, first, personal writing and, then, for literary and/or other research writing.

For you, each story provides multiple diagnostic and assessment tools that can be easily collected and graded. The book is perforated and the pedagogy is purposefully consistent, so that you have the option of assigning each story classwide or assigning each story on an individualized basis. Please note that, unless you have consistently advanced classes, the selections in Chapter Five are, in fact, intended for individualization for the exceptional, advancing student. As diagnostic tools, the pre-reading vocabulary work provides insight into student word mastery, while the post-reading journal and later follow-up questions and the discussion questions provide insight into student comprehension. As assessment tools, any combinations of the above can be collected for grading. Also, please note that each entry in this manual starts with general suggestions for each story and then lists all potential vocabulary words, so that you can select specific words to reinforce other vocabulary studies, should you wish to do so. Please note, also, that we have deleted potentially offensive words in text, wherever feasible.

Related to assessment, the vocabulary definitions, which are self-explanatory, and the objective questions have clear right-and-wrong answers. However, the answers provided in this manual, except for the objective questions, are "suggested." The student is working with literature and is providing written answers. I have provided general parameters here, but student answers will certainly, and often delightfully, vary.

"How *I* Use This Book," located in the book's Appendix, is also intended to offer you some teaching options.

The ultimate intent of this book is to bring American literature to the budding reader. The pedagogy is designed to involve the student in the reading, thereby making each story more accessible, while simultaneously providing you with multiple, efficient diagnostic and assessment tools.

I *sincerely* hope you and your students enjoy using this book as much as I have enjoyed developing it.

Yvonne Collioud Sisko

# CHAPTER ONE

## *CHARACTERS and Conflicts*

## "A WORN PATH"

An often asked question is whether the grandson is alive or dead. Welty herself has stated that she has been surprised by this question. Seeing an old woman crossing a winter landscape inspired this story; Welty gave the old woman she saw a reason for her journey. In this, the boy being alive validates Old Phoenix's journey, persistence, and love. And the story is, after all, about the journey, both the described one there and the assumed one back, and about unwavering love.

**Vocabulary. Words crucial to understanding the story are presented in *Pre-reading Vocabulary—Context.*** However, all potentially troublesome words are listed here in the order they appear in the text, so that (1) you can easily identify words you may wish to stress and (2) you can locate them easily in the text.

# Vocabulary – "A WORN PATH"

1. pendulum
2. grave
3. persistent
4. meditative
5. apron
6. bleached
7. illuminated
8. frailest
9. quivering
10. thicket
11. cane
12. limber
13. switch
14. rouse
15. hollow
16. severe
17. thorny
18. trembling
19. stoop
20. trial
21. fiercely
22. festival
23. parade
24. mistletoe
25. withered
26. buzzard
27. furrow
28. bull
29. maze
30. ragged
31. scarecrow
32. strutting
33. husks
34. whirled
35. quail
36. dainty
37. spring
38. alligator
39. lolling
40. mediating
41. growling
42. yonder
43. radiation
44. nickel
45. erect
46. utterly
47. bound
48. inclined
49. steeple
50. Natchez
51. tower
52. document
53. ceremonial
54. charity
55. history
56. twitch
57. clockwork
58. trace
59. upright
60. solemn
61. rigidity
62. medicine
63. armour
64. flicker
65. comprehension
66. frowned
67. dignified
68. forgiveness
69. surrender
70. lye
71. obstinate
72. patch
73. quilt
74. enduring
75. windmill

## Journal Answers

*MLA Works Cited.*

Welty, Eudora. "A Worn Path." <u>American 24-Karat Gold</u>. 2nd ed. Ed. Yvonne
      Sisko. New York: Longman, 2007. 28–35.

*Main Character(s).* Old Phoenix, the poor, aged, and determined lady, is the sole
main character in this character study.

*Supporting Characters.* The grandson, the dog, the hunter and his dog, the lady
on the street, the attendant, the nurse, and the implied doctor are all part of Old
Phoenix's journey.

*Setting.* Set in the south (alligator reference) along the Natchez Trace (an old
native path linking Natchez, Mississippi with Nashville, Tennessee), the story
can be placed along any arduous path.

*Sequence. Here is an informal outline, but answers will vary.*

  I. Journey.
     A. She walks through the woods.
     B. She walks through the thicket.
     C. She crosses the log over the creek.
     D. She goes over the barbed-wire fence.
     E. She passes through the cotton field with the scarecrow.
     F. She meets the dog and the hunter and gains the nickel.

 II. Natchez.
     A. She meets the lady who ties her shoe.
     B. She meets the attendant in the doctor's office.
     C. She meets the nurse in the doctor's office.
     D. She gets the medicine.
     E. She gets another nickel.

III. Journey back.
     A. She is off to buy a windmill.
     B. She is off to return home.

*Plot. With a two-sentence limit, answers will vary.*
An old woman faces challenges when she goes to get medicine for her grandson.

*Conflicts.* Human v. nature is relevant in Old Phoenix's struggle to get there.
Human v. society and/or poverty is relevant in Old Phoenix's desire for nickels.

*Significant Quotations.*

  a. This indicates that while Old Phoenix is poor, right down to the "apron of bleached sugar sacks," she is proud and feels she is dressed in her best to go to town.

b. This refers to the meeting with the hunter who pulls her out of the ditch and scares the dog away. It also indicates her interest in what little money she needs; she slyly picks up the nickel he drops while he is chasing the bothersome dog away. This also indicates a trial on her journey.

c. This indicates that Phoenix has finally arrived in town, old though she may be.

d. This refers to her history with the doctor's office and the very reason for her journey. She infrequently comes to town to get medicine for her grandson's throat that was injured by lye, a medicine which she does not pay for.

e. This summarizes what she will do with the two nickels, one "stolen" from the hunter and the other donated by the attendant, and infers the continuing love for her grandson.

## Follow-up Questions. 10 Short Questions

*These are intended for objective assessment and focus on comprehension only, purposely avoiding literary controversy.*

1. b   She is rather poorly dressed, "apron of bleached sugar sacks" and all.

2. c   She is very concerned, considers herself well-dressed, and fights hard with the thorns not to ruin her clothes.

3. c   The hunter drops the nickel and Old Phoenix stealthily picks it up. He certainly does not hand it to her and there is no indication that he drops it on purpose.

4. a   Following up 3, Old Phoenix stealthily pockets the coin while the hunter is not looking.

5. a   The base of the story centers around the rigors of her journey.

6. b   We witness the journey, and the hunter and the nurse comment on the length of her trip.

7. a   The nurse is very familiar with her and lets the reader know Old Phoenix is there several times each year.

8. c   The nurse marks "'charity'"; this is testing both recognizing that Old Phoenix does not pay and the definition for "charity," a context vocabulary word.

9. a   She gladly accepts assistance from the hunter, the lady, the nurse, and the attendant.

10. b  Clothing, picking up a stray nickel, accepting charity, and the very nature of her journey on foot all clearly imply her material poverty.

### Follow-up Questions. 5 Significant Quotations

*These are highly focused and are intended for short answer subjective assessment of comprehension only, purposely avoiding literary controversy.*

1. This identifies just one of the many obstacles on her long and challenging trip.
2. This refers to the story with the hunter who scares off a stray dog and drops a nickel which Old Phoenix retrieves while he is not looking.
3. This indicates her journey has been successful and she has reached the city.
4. This refers to the scene in the doctor's office wherein Old Phoenix receives, at no cost, medication for her grandson's throat injured by lye.
5. This indicates what Old Phoenix will buy for her grandson with the nickels (one retrieved from the hunter and one donated by the attendant), and infers her continuing love for her grandson.

### Follow-up Questions. 2 Comprehension Essay Questions

*These are highly focused and are intended for subjective assessment of comprehension only, purposely avoiding literary controversy or ancillary opinions. Intended to draw upon all facets of the story, 1 and 2 may repeat and/or complement each other.*

1. This asks the student to focus on Old Phoenix's unwavering determination. As she stumbles, she arises. The student should discuss the creek, the hunter who supplies her with a fortuitous nickel, the trek through town and to the doctor's office that supplies her with free medicine and even a coin to buy a gift for her grandson. She survives her arduous journey and is the better for it.
2. The title summarizes the story of the journey. The student should note the specific difficulties of the trip and that this is a route well known to Old Phoenix.

### Discussion Questions

*Unlike the Follow-up Questions which are intended to measure comprehension only, thereby avoiding personal opinions and/or literary controversy, these questions are intended to elicit opinions and/or debate. Answers here are only suggestions as the literary discussion may take many forms.*

# Journal Answers

*MLA Works Cited.*

Gonzalez-Wippler, Migene. "Yoruba." <u>American 24-Karat Gold</u>. 2nd ed. Ed. Yvonne Sisko. New York: Longman, 2007. 44–53.

*Main Character(s).* The central characters in this story are the narrator and María. The narrator tells the story of her experiences during her childhood just before she is to attend school. María is the nanny who is hired to care for the child, adores the child, and introduces the child to Santeria rituals.

*Supporting Characters.* The first supporting characters the reader meets are the child's family and include the parents and grandparents. The mother, in particular, does not approve of María to begin with, but then comes to accept her because of the child's love for her. Other characters include the implied people in town and the bus driver who takes the narrator and María to the beach. The drowned boy, his family, and the police and lifeguards are all supporting characters in the drowning story that gives insight into the religious rites. At the base of these rituals is Yemaya, the adapted form of the Catholic Virgin Mother.

*Setting.* The story is set in Puerto Rico. It could conceivably be moved to another island or even beach location, although the religious rites limit the locations.

*Sequence. Here is an informal outline, but answers will vary.*

   I. María becomes the nanny.
     A. She cares for the narrator.
     B. She takes the narrator everywhere.

  II. The narrator is going to go to school.
     A. Her family plans a party.
     B. María takes the narrator to protect her.

 III. María takes the narrator to the beach.
     A. The narrator is stripped of her old clothes/old ways.
     B. The narrator is trimmed in syrup, given seven pennies, and placed in the water.
     C. The wave takes the sugarcane syrup and the pennies.
     D. The narrator is protected.

 IV. The mother retrieves her lost son.
     A. The mother offers four candles to the sea.
     B. The son's body is returned.

  V. The narrator is ready to celebrate her birthday and to go to school.

*Plot. With a two-sentence limit, answers will vary.*
A woman offers a child with gifts to the sea to protect the child.

*Conflicts.* Human v. human is relevant in, first, the mother's misgivings about María and, then, in the conflict between María and the narrator when the narrator is afraid at the beach. Human v. nature is relevant when the beach setting and then the tide originally scare the narrator. Human v. nature is also relevant in the story of the drowning. Human v. society is relevant in the narrator's initial reluctance to accept the rituals presented by the religion. Human v. society is also relevant in the drowning story in the mother's resistance to the advice of the police.

*Significant Quotations.*

    a. The student should describe the little girl, who is the narrator, and María, who is the colorful and dedicated nanny. The student should note that these are the central characters in this story.

    b. The student should note that this is the point at which María must take action. The narrator is going to go to school and María will now set out to protect the narrator.

    c. The student should describe the ritual at the beach, wherein the narrator meets Yemaya entering the water sideways, clad in syrup, and with pennies to offer.

    d. The student should describe the story of the lost boy and the mother who seeks Yemaya's help in returning her boy with the candle offering.

    e. The student should explain that María has performed this ritual in order to protect the narrator as she goes to school.

## Follow-up Questions. 10 Short Questions
*These are intended for objective assessment and focus on comprehension only, purposely avoiding literary controversy.*

    1. c    This identifies María's role and is central to understanding the characters.

    2. b    The luxuries at home (new clothes, an employed nanny, etc.) all indicate a family of means. There is no indication of a farm but rather of a city home where the bus, market, etc. are all accessible.

    3. a    María is describe as being "colorful" and is very "lively" in her activities and travels. She is certainly not "quiet" and is, in fact, so colorful that the narrator's mother is not sure if she is the right person to be a nanny.

4. a   Again, María is clearly described as a large person with "voluminous skirts" and much breadth.

5. c   It is important that the student has picked up this literal detail. María takes the narrator to mass and certainly considers herself a devoted Catholic. She sees no conflict between Catholicism and her more tribal rites.

6. a   This focuses the student on the symbol of the ritual. The narrator is stripped of her old clothes to strip her of her old ways. Further, she is told not to confront the water, which is an insult, and awaits the water sideward. Her new clothes are reserved for her party.

7. c   All part of the ritual, the syrup is a sweet offering the Yemaya. The narrator balks at the stickiness of it. Although it is theoretically "good for her" as part of the ritual, the offering to Yemaya is the best answer here.

8. b   It is critical to understanding the story that the ritual is done out of love and is intended to protect the narrator. Drowning might indicate confusion with the story of the boy's drowning.

9. c   Again looking for accurate comprehension of literal details, the boy's body is returned and it is returned for four candles. The seven pennies are what the narrator offers.

10. b   The student must infer that the ritual at the beach is prompted by love. María has no revenge or hatred for the narrator and clearly adores her.

## Follow-up Questions. 5 Significant Quotations
*These are highly focused and are intended for short answer subjective assessment of comprehension only, purposely avoiding literary controversy.*

1. The student should discuss the two main characters here. The person speaking is the narrator as a child and the center of the story's rituals. María is the nanny who adores the little narrator. The student may comment on the mother's reservations and María's flamboyant personality.

2. The student should explain that it is this birthday and the coming of school attendance that prompt María to take the little narrator to the beach for the protection ritual.

3. The student should explain the ritual at the beach. Here, the wave has enveloped the narrator. The sweet syrup and the seven pennies were all offerings at the ritual.

4. The student should relate the story of the boy's drowning. The boy drowns and no one can find his body. His mother goes to sea and offers four can-

dles where he disappeared and his body reappears. This story-within-a-story is used to help explain the offerings to Yemaya.

5.  The student should explain that with the washing of the wave and the sweet syrup and pennies taken, María feels that she has now placed the narrator in Yemaya's protection.

## Follow-up Questions. 2 Comprehension Essay Questions

*These are highly focused and are intended for subjective assessment of comprehension only, purposely avoiding literary controversy and/or ancillary opinions. Intended to draw upon all facets of the story, 1 and 2 may repeat and/or complement each other.*

1.  These offer the student an interesting study. Here, the student will want to describe María's *bon vivant* adventures and colorful religion. The student will need to describe María's devotion to the narrator and her belief that the ritual at beach will protect the narrator.

2.  Here, the student will need to take the narrator's point of view. The student will need to describe the narrator's love for María and her colorful ways. The student will need to note the narrator's trust in María. And the student will need to describe the mixture of fear and serenity, distrust and trust during the beachside ritual.

## Discussion Questions

*Unlike the Follow-up Questions which are intended to measure comprehension only, thereby avoiding personal opinions and/or literary controversy, these questions are intended to elicit opinions and/or debate. Answers here are only suggestions as the literary discussion may take many forms.*

1.  Depending on your class matrix, this discussion may go in many directions. Certainly, this ritual is very similar to Christian baptism. The idea of making offerings to God or gods occurs in many religions. Combining God or gods with nature dates back to animism, the earliest known form of human worship, and is found in many religions.

2.  This calls for students to think back and even to refer back to the story. Yemaya is the emanation of the Catholic Virgin Mother and is a being central to the story. However, according to María, the belief in Yemaya comes from the brave tribe called the Yoruba. The Yoruba are African and it is the combination of their beliefs and Catholicism that are at the core of the rituals.

Puerto Rican people refer to African concepts as "Yoruba" and to the combined, Latin American practice as "Santeria," but students may not know this distinction.

# "THE SECRET LIFE OF WALTER MITTY"

In this classic tale, Thurber presents a character study through heroic dreams in a mundane, suburban existence. Of course, humor requires knowledge and many will miss the "initiative and referendum" barb, but once students tune into the daydream nature of this reading, they usually enjoy and even identify with the story. The many quotes and/or conversations make this challenging but lively reading.

**Vocabulary. Words crucial to understanding the story are presented in *Pre-reading Vocabulary—Context.*** However, all potentially troublesome words are listed here in the order they appear in the text, so that (1) you can easily identify words you may wish to stress and (2) you can locate them easily in the text.

# Vocabulary – "THE SECRET LIFE OF WALTER MITTY"

1. commander
2. uniform
3. braided
4. rakish
5. spoiling (vb.)
6. lieutenant
7. rev
8. cylinder
9. pilot
10. complicated
11. dial
12. auxiliary
13. turret
14. crew
15. hurtling
16. hydroplane
17. shock
18. astonishment
19. grossly
20. fade
21. remote
22. intimate
23. tense
24. hastily
25. lurch
26. aimless
27. specialist
28. corridor
29. distraught
30. haggard
31. Roosevelt
32. brilliant
33. tertiary
34. complicated
35. anaesthetizer
36. intern
37. delicately
38. glistening
39. faulty
40. piston
41. craven
42. adjust
43. jam (vb.)
44. attendant
45. mutter
46. cautiously
47. ignition
48. vault (vb.)
49. insolent
50. wound
51. axle
52. sling
53. slush
54. carborundum
55. initiative
56. referendum
57. thrust
58. automatic
59. calmly
60. rap (vb.)
61. attorney
62. insinuating
63. objection
64. bickering
65. pandemonium
66. bedlam
67. savagely
68. cur
69. biscuit
70. ruined
71. cannonading
72. sergeant
73. captain
74. tousle
75. wearily
76. anxious
77. ammunition
78. whine
79. dugout
80. batter (vb.)
81. rend
82. faint
83. fleeting
84. kilometre
85. vague
86. revolving
87. derisive
88. sleet
89. scornful
90. disdainful
91. inscrutable

**Journal Answers**

*MLA Works Cited.*

Thurber, James. "The Secret Life of Walter Mitty." <u>American 24-Karat Gold</u>. 2nd ed. Ed. Yvonne Sisko. New York: Longman, 2007. 62–66.

*Main Character(s).* The central character in this story is Walter Mitty, the seemingly innocuous husband who daydreams himself in heroic roles.

*Supporting Characters.* Mrs. Mitty, of course, is there throughout to awaken him from the daydreams. The navy subordinate, the policeman, the doctors, the parking-lot attendant, the newspaper boy, the attorney, the ladies on the street who observe him, and the sergeant are supporting in either inspiring, participating in, or awakening Mitty from his daydreams.

*Setting.* Set in a town called Waterbury, the story can take place in any small town with enough characters to inspire fantasies.

*Sequence. Here is an informal outline, but answers will vary.*

  I. Dream about being a Navy hydroplane commander.
     A. Mitty is driving his car.
     B. Wife wakes him telling him to slow down.

 II. Dream about being a surgeon.
     A. Mitty takes off his gloves.
     B. Mitty drives past the hospital.
     C. Mitty becomes a surgeon and mechanic who saves the day.
     D. In reality, Mitty feels inferior about changing tire chains.

III. Dreams about being a trial witness.
     A. Paperboy shouts out headlines about a local trial.
     B. Mitty becomes a star witness and crack shot.
     C. In reality, Mitty set out to buy puppy biscuits.

 IV. Dreams about being a bomber pilot.
     A. Mitty reads an article on World War II planes while waiting for his wife.
     B. Mitty becomes Captain Mitty who will solo a bomber over Germany.
     C. Wife's tap wakes him.

  V. Dreams about facing a firing squad.
     A. Wife stops at the drugstore and he lights a cigarette.
     B. Mitty becomes a hero in front of a firing squad.
     C. Mitty is "inscrutable to the end."

*Plot. With a three-sentence limit, answers will vary.*
Man fills his mundane life with heroic daydreams.

*Conflicts.* Human v. society applies in Mitty's silent argument with his lot in life. Human v. human is possible in his rather unsympathetic wife. However in his dreams, human v. himself or human v. society do not apply; this is the relief of his conflict with his lot in society.

*Significant Quotations.*

a. Mitty has just been dreaming that he is a Navy hydroplane commander and Mrs. Mitty brings him back to earth, telling him he is driving the family car too fast.

b. This inspires the next dream when he becomes a renown surgeon who mechanically and medically saves the day.

c. This inspires the next dream when he becomes a star witness and expert shot.

d. This inspires the next dream when he becomes a bomber pilot setting out on a heroic, solo mission in World War II.

e. This summarizes the many dreams that make up Mitty's secret, day dreaming, fantasy world.


## Follow-up Questions. 10 Short Questions

*These are intended for objective assessment and focus on comprehension only, purposely avoiding literary controversy.*

1. c   Mitty is only dreaming. This question measures if the student has understood the story's central thought. This is the heart of the story and is retested several times.

2. b   Mrs. Mitty seems to give the orders here; it can be inferred that this is, in fact, an incentive for the dreams.

3. a   The gloves lead into the surgeon scenario. Even if the student does not memorize the story—and there's a good deal to be said against mere memorization—the student familiar with the story will be able to solve this by reading on. This is true of questions 6 and 9 also, which also test working familiarity.

4. c   Mitty is not the renown surgeon he dreams he is. Again, this question measures if the student has understood the story's central thought.

5. b   In real life, Mitty sheds the gloves his wife instructs him to wear.

6. a   To be used with 7 (please see 3), overshoes inspire nothing; only "a" is relevant. Students accustom to this format rapidly, which demands closer test reading on their part.

7. b   The newsboy in 6 inspires the trial dream in 7. Mitty is neither on trial nor a lawyer in real life.

8. c   Mitty is again daydreaming. Again, this question measures if the student has understood the story's central thought.

9. c   The *Liberty* article leads to the World War II bomber pilot dream (please see 3).

10. c   Mitty is again daydreaming. Again, this question measures if the student has understood the story's central thought.

## Follow-up Questions. 5 Significant Quotations

*These are highly focused and intended for short answer subjective assessment of comprehension only, purposely avoiding literary controversy.*

1. This indicates the mix between dreaming he was a Navy hydroplane commander and really driving to Waterbury. The student should note this mix of reality and dreams.

2. The "Dr." in the phrase indicates that we are in the surgeon dream, which the student should be able to describe.

3. The "gun" indicates we are in the trial dream, which the student should be able to describe.

4. This is the article that leads into the bomber pilot dream, which the student should be able to describe.

5. This wonderful phrase, said by Mitty to his wife, sums up his place in reality and in their relationship; yes, he is the thinker, ever off on fantasies, while she is the pragmatist, rooted in routine and reality, who does not recognize his dreaming.

## Follow-up Questions. 2 Comprehension Essay Questions

*These are highly focused and are intended for subjective assessment of comprehension only, purposely avoiding literary controversy or ancillary opinions.*

*Intended to draw upon all facets of the story, 1 and 2 may repeat and/or complement each other.*

1. The title is fundamental to the story. The daydreams are Mitty's "Secret Life." The student should explain the daydreams used to escape mundane reality and then should use each (the dashing Navy lieutenant, the renown surgeon, the sensational trial witness, the heroic bomber pilot) to demonstrate the mental escapes.

2. Answers will vary greatly here. The student should use the wife's bossiness and Mitty's daydreams as substantiation for each description.

## Discussion Questions

*Unlike the Follow-up Questions which are intended to measure comprehension only, thereby avoiding personal opinions and/or literary controversy, these questions are intended to elicit opinions and/or debate. Answers here are only suggestions as the literary discussion may take many forms.*

1. This encourages lively discourse. There are many daydreams to choose from and this focuses the students on the imagined events in the story.

2. This encourages imagination and inference. After reading, many have pictures in their minds of both Mitty and his wife. The students can be encouraged to substantiate their images with details from the story.

## "THE TELL-TALE HEART"

Often abridged for high schoolers, here we have one of Poe's classics in his wonderful and formal language. Because the story draws the reader deeper and deeper into the world of the insane mind, you may want to discuss protagonist and antagonist with students. You may also want to discuss the practice of the time of elderly or wealthy people adopting younger people and even protégés. You may find students who assume the narrator is a female and even an abused and sympathetic female, in this day-and-age of overt discussions on abuse, thereby missing the point of the grisly homicide. While the formal language is challenging, the mere interest of the story carries along almost all readers.

**Vocabulary. Words crucial to understanding the story are presented in** *Pre-reading Vocabulary—Context.* However, all potentially troublesome words are listed in the order they appear in the text, so that (1) you can easily identify words you may wish to stress and (2) you can locate them easily in the text.

# Vocabulary – "THE TELL-TALE HEART"

1. dreadful
2. sharpen
3. dull
4. hearken
5. conceive
6. haunt
7. object
8. vulture
9. mad
10. caution
11. foresight
12. dissimulation
13. sufficient
14. lantern
15. cunning
16. disturb
17. hinges
18. courageous
19. hearty
20. profound
21. sagacity
22. scarcely
23. triumph
24. chuckle
25. startle
26. shutters
27. groan
28. mortal
29. terror
30. grief
31. stifle
32. awe
33. pity
34. slight
35. supposition
36. vain
37. stalk
38. mournful
39. influence
40. perceive
41. crevice
42. stealth
43. dim
44. furious
45. distinct
46. instinct
47. damned
48. enveloped
49. fury
50. stimulate
51. refrain
52. scarcely
53. tattoo
54. anxiety
55. shriek
56. gaily
57. deed
58. muffle
59. vex
60. cease
61. corpse
62. pulsation
63. conceal
64. wane
65. dismember
66. chamber
67. deposit
68. scantling
69. detect
70. suavity
71. suspicion
72. foul
73. arouse
74. lodge
75. depute
76. premises
77. treasure
78. enthusiasm
79. fatigue
80. audacity
81. singularly
82. definitive
83. fluently
84. gasp
85. vehemently
86. gesticulation
87. stride
88. rave
89. mockery
90. agony
91. derision
92. hypocritical
93. hideous

**Journal Answers**

*MLA Works Cited.*

Poe, Edgar Allan. "The Tell-Tale Heart." <u>American 24-Karat Gold</u>. 2nd ed. Ed. Yvonne Sisko. New York: Longman, 2007. 75–79.

*Main Character(s).* The narrator is unquestionably the central character. Students may also defend the old man as a main character and central to the action.

*Supporting Characters.* If not discussed as a main character, the old man is certainly a supporting character. The neighbors who call the police and the police themselves who witness the confession are also supporting characters.

*Setting.* Set in a home close enough for neighbors to hear a ruckus, any home might do. The major component of setting in any Poe story is, of course, the dark and suspenseful mood.

*Sequence. Here is an informal outline, but answers may vary.*

  I. The setup.
      A. The narrator loves the old man.
      B. The narrator keeps discussing his "disease."

 II. The aggression.
      A. The narrator hates the eye.
      B. The narrator stalks the man for seven nights.

III. The eighth night and the murder.
      A. The eye is closed and the narrator smothers the old man.
      B. The narrator dismembers the old man and buries his parts under the floor planks.
      C. The neighbors call the police.

 IV. The tell-tale heart.
      A. The police arrive to check on a noise.
      B. The narrator invites them in to chat casually.
      C. During the chat, the narrator hears the dead heart beating.
      D. The narrator, in a flurry of rage, confesses to the murder.

*Plot. With a two-sentence limit, answers will vary.*

An insane man becomes obsessed with an old man's eye and, after planning, kills and then dismembers the old man, only to confess to the police shortly after their arrival.

*Conflicts.* Certainly human v. human is involved as the narrator kills the old man. Certainly human v. himself is involved as the narrator's insanity overcomes him.

Possible human v. society is involved in the tension the police cause in the narrator.

*Significant Quotations.*

   a. This is not only a clear mention of the narrator's insanity, but is also a piece of his continuing apologetic, trying to convince the reader that he is not mad.

   b. This is the stated reason for the murder; the narrator loves the old man but cannot stand his eye.

   c. "Eighth" indicates (1) the seven nights before of stalking and (2) the night of the murder. Students should discuss this whole scenario.

   d. This is the tell-tale heart. Students should discuss the dismemberment and the narrator's madness.

   e. "Officers" indicates this is approaching the moment of confession.

## Follow-up Questions. 10 Short Questions

*These are intended for objective assessment and focus on comprehension only, purposely avoiding literary controversy.*

   1. a   He goes to great lengths to prove not only how sane he is, but also how extraordinarily clever he thinks he is. He considers himself better than normal, so "sane" is the best choice here.

   2. c   Again, he goes to great lengths to convince the reader of his sanity and his cleverness. "C" is the *best* choice here.

   3. a   He openly tells us he loves the old man and is kind during his waking hours.

   4. b   Prior discussion about adoption practices might help students here, but even without that discussion the narrator clearly tells us that he looks on the old man as a father.

   5. c   Again, prior discussion about adoption practices would make this clearer to the student. However, even without prior explanation a family relationship is certainly inferred.

   6. b   The narrator clearly tells us he loves the old man; this is a necessary component of the insanity theme and retests this fundamental fact—that the narrator kills someone he loves.

   7. a   The eye is the sole incentive the narrator offers and the eye must be open to kill the old man he loves. It is the core of the obsession and is fundamental to understanding the insanity.

8. a   Not only does he take the reader through each step of his careful planning, but he continually tells us how clever his planning is.

9. c   Asked because this is fundamental to the student understanding the distortion of the insanity, the old man is dead so his heart cannot beat and the only one who hears it is the narrator; the police cannot hear a dead heart and the old man is dead.

10. a   There is no literal indication that the police suspect the narrator. His confession is the logical result of his madness.

## Follow-up Questions. 5 Significant Quotations

*These are highly focused and are intended for short answer subjective assessment of comprehension only, purposely avoiding literary controversy.*

1. This refers to the narrator's preoccupation with his madness; he repeatedly rationalizes for himself and for the reader that he is sane.

2. This is the obsession and the very reason for the murder. The student should explain that the narrator loved the old man but became obsessed with the eye.

3. Again, the narrator discusses his sanity and the student should comment on the logical, if diabolical, planning.

4. This notes, again, the planning seven nights before and brings us to the brink of the murder; the student should note that once the eye is open, the murder occurs.

5. This is the moment of confession. The student should discuss the murder ("deed"), dismemberment ("tear up the planks"), and the insanity ("the beating of his hideous heart").

## Follow-up Questions. 2 Comprehension Essay Questions

*These are highly focused and are intended for subjective assessment of comprehension only, purposely avoiding literary controversy and ancillary opinions. Intended to draw upon all facets of the story, 1 and 2 may repeat and/or complement each other.*

1. The title is central to the story. The student should relate the events in sequence with the imagined heartbeat resulting in the confession.

2. The confession summarizes the story's events. The student should relate the events in sequence that lead to the ultimate events in the confession.

**Discussion Questions**

*Unlike the Follow-up Questions which are intended to measure comprehension only, thereby avoiding personal opinions and/or literary controversy, these questions are intended to elicit opinions and/or debate. Answers here are only suggestions as the literary discussion may take many forms.*

1. A definition of "homicidal mind" may be necessary here. Then students should be encouraged to focus on the premeditation and subsequent cover-up. Lively debate usually ensues as students discuss why he confessed.

2. This calls for close reading of the biographical blurb. Poe's adoption and problems with his adoptive father, his misbehaviors, and his addiction obsession are all good grounds for discussion related to this story.

# "THERE WILL COME SOFT RAINS"

In this stirring Bradbury tale, non-characters (the bomb, the house, the robots, even the energy of fire) become the characters, and traditional characters (the family and the dog) become setting and props that enhance the action. In this succinct dialectic, Bradbury argues that the very machines we create will destroy us. Students enjoy and are even moved by this story, but often need several readings to understand the situation.

**Vocabulary. Words crucial to understanding the story are presented in *Prereading Vocabulary—Context*.** However, all potentially troublesome words are listed here in the order they appear in the text, so that (1) you can easily identify words you may wish to stress and (2) you can locate them easily in the text.

# Vocabulary – "THERE WILL COME SOFT RAINS"

1. hiss
2. sigh
3. eject
4. interior
5. anniversary
6. insurance
7. relay (n.)
8. glide
9. tread
10. echo
11. chime
12. shrivel
13. wedge
14. emerge
15. twinkling
16. warren
17. robot
18. knead
19. mysterious
20. invader
21. burrow
22. rubble
23. ashes
24. radioactive
25. sprinkler
26. fount
27. char
28. silhouette
29. image
30. titanic
31. charcoal
32. inquire
33. old maid
34. preoccupation
35. mechanical
36. paranoia
37. quiver
38. startle
39. attendant
40. choir
41. ritual
42. recognize
43. huge
44. fleshy
45. inconvenience
46. fragment
47. offending
48. miniature
49. vent (n.)
50. incinerator
51. Baal
52. hysterical
53. yelp
54. froth
55. frenzy
56. decay
57. regiment
58. patio
59. martini
60. antelope
61. panther
62. cavort
63. fantasy
64. sprocket
65. meadow
66. bellow
67. okapi
68. dissolve
69. parch
70. manipulate
71. hearth
72. circuit
73. preference
74. swallow (n.)
75. shimmer
76. tremulous
77. whim
78. perish
79. utterly
80. mound
81. bough
82. solvent
83. linoleum
84. ease
85. scurry
86. pistol (vb.)
87. shrug
88. quench
89. cease
90. reserve
91. crackle
92. Picasso
93. Matisse
94. delicacy
95. canvas
96. reinforcement
97. attic
98. faucet
99. chemical
100. venom
101. shatter
102. shrapnel
103. shudder
104. skeleton
105. cringe
106. surgeon
107. capillary
108. scald

109. brittle
110. wail
111. tragic
112. sheathing
113. jungle
114. avalanche
115. oblivious
116. frantic
117. insane
118. maniac
119. unity
120. horrid
121. sublime
122. disregard
123. wither
124. timber
125. psychopathic
126. cellar
127. clutter
128. dawn

# Journal Answers

*MLA Works Cited.*

Bradbury, Ray. "There Will Come Soft Rains." <u>American 24-Karat Gold</u>. 2nd ed. Ed. Yvonne Sisko. New York: Longman, 2007. 88–92.

*Main Character(s).* Certainly the "mice" or robots, and even the house *per se* and the bomb, may be argued as main characters.

*Supporting Characters.* The wind, the branch, the solvent, the fire, the incinerator, the individual robots, and the bomb may be argued as supporting characters. The family, who built the house but who are now left only in silhouette, and the dying dog are supporting characters in this theme of mechanical annihilation.

*Setting.* The setting is the scene after atomic devastation. Set in California, this could be set anywhere atomic annihilation might occur.

*Sequence. Here is an informal outline, but answers will vary.*

I. Morning.
  A. Breakfast is made.
  B. Day's schedule is announced.
  C. Garage door opens and closes.
  D. Breakfast is cleared.
  E. Robots clean the house.
  F. The sprinklers water the lawn.

II. The bomb (flashback).
  A. There is a radioactive glow.
  B. The family is silhouetted against the wall.

III. The dog.
  A. The dog enters and despairingly goes mad.
  B. The dog dies.
  C. The dog is swept away and incinerated.

IV. Afternoon.
  A. Bridge game is set up on the patio and cleared.
  B. The nursery is barren.

V. Evening.
  A. The bath is filled.
  B. The dinner is cooked.
  C. The beds are warmed.
  D. A poem is read.

VI. The house dies at night.
   A. Wind sends a branch through the kitchen window knocking over a solvent bottle.
   B. The kitchen catches on fire.
   C. A pump stops and the house burns.
   D. Fire kills the house's "brain" and all the machines die and the house finally collapses.
VII. Next day, one last voice announces the date.

*Plot. With a three-sentence limit, answers will vary.*
An atomic bomb explodes, destroying a family and their home.
*Conflicts.* Bradbury's conflict is very focused: human v. machines/science/technology. The machines win.
*Significant Quotations.*

   a. This indicates the atomic bomb and the student should discuss the bomb and the devastation it has left.
   b. In this surreal and moving portrait, the student should discuss the demise of the family.
   c. This refers to the robots, "mice," or house machines and the student should discuss this automated house.
   d. This selection from the poem may require some discussion. Bradbury here is implying that, although we have created machines which have killed us, the natural world will go on. It is the one shred of hope in this otherwise desolate tale.
   e. This is the moment at which the fire will start to win and the house will start to die.

**Follow-up Questions. 10 Short Questions**
*These are intended for objective assessment and focus on comprehension only, purposely avoiding literary controversy.*

   1. b   While Bradbury uses the term "mice," these are, in fact, the house robots. This question checks to see if the student has understood the figurative illusion. Further and related to testing techniques, since "animals" and "rodents" basically cancel each other out, this teaches the student that when two answers cancel each other out in testing, another answer is often the right answer.

2. c    This is fundamental to the story and student understanding as the story is all about the house doing everything on its own.

3. b    This reinforces 3; the house and/or its machines doing everything on its own is fundamental to the story.

4. b    Again a reinforcement to 2 and 3; the student must understand that the house is doing the work.

5. c    The family is dead, not dying. Further, instructions call for the best answer, and the most accurate answer here is that they have been vaporized by the bomb.

6. c    Again, best answer is the bomb; while there is a fire, the fire is an indirect result of the bomb that caused all this destruction.

7. a    Testing simple literal recall, the dog becomes ill and dies.

8. a    He is neither fed nor buried, but rather incinerated. This coincidentally checks if the student understands "incinerator," a pre-reading context word.

9. b    By morning the house is ashes which infers it has burned to the ground.

10. a    The poem offers the one ray of hope in the story in, "And Spring herself, when she woke at dawn/ Would scarcely know that we were gone."

## Follow-up Questions. 5 Significant Quotations

*These are highly focused and are intended for short answer subjective assessment of comprehension only, purposely avoiding literary controversy.*

1. This refers to the atomic bomb and the student should discuss the atomic blast that sets up this story.

2. This refers to the automated house aid. The student should discuss the mechanical amenities.

3. This refers to the family and the student should discuss that, as a result of the bomb, the family has been vaporized and now is nothing but silhouettes on the wall.

4. This is the poem the house reads to no one, *albeit* the missing family, and this passage offers Bradbury's one ray of hope in this story of destruction.

5. This is the moment the house starts to die. The student should discuss the significance of the falling solvent which ignites the kitchen and ultimately destroys the house as the machines start to fail.

**Follow-up Questions. 2 Comprehension Essay Questions**

*These are highly focused and are intended for subjective assessment of comprehension only, purposely avoiding literary controversy and ancillary opinions. Intended to draw upon all facets of the story, 1 and 2 may repeat and/or complement each other.*

1. The student should discuss the destruction directly related to the bomb (the family's incineration, the dog's demise, the continual failure of the house, etc.). The more astute may also discuss the relevance of the poem.

2. The student should discuss all the destruction, both by the bomb of man and by the house machinery of man. The more astute may also discuss the relevance of the poem.

**Discussion Questions**

*Unlike the Follow-up Questions which are intended to measure comprehension only, thereby avoiding personal opinions and/or literary controversy, these questions are intended to elicit opinions and/or debate. Answers here are only suggestions as the literary discussion may take many forms.*

1. Bradbury's central thesis is twofold: war created by humans will kill us and the machines created by humans will kill us. This affords a good discussion on narrative thesis and focuses students on the images presented in this story.

2. This is an extension of the above and a very doable application of the dialectic dynamic. Humankind is the given and humankind produces war (the antithesis) which then destroys humankind (synthesis). Humankind is the given and humankind produces machines (the antithesis) which then destroy humankind (synthesis). This offers rich discussion in both the dialectic and the events in the story.

# CHAPTER TWO

## *SETTING and Props*

# "BONE GIRL"

This is a most interesting story that combines the observations of Joseph Bruchac, of Abenaki Native American heritage, with very eerie tales. It is down-to-earth yet supernatural and is readable for all students.

**Vocabulary. Words crucial to understanding the story are presented in *Pre-reading Vocabulary—Context.*** However, all potentially troublesome words are listed here in the order they appear in the text, so that (1) you can easily identify words you may wish to stress and (2) you can locate them easily in the text.

# Vocabulary – "BONE GIRL"

1. abandoned
2. quarry
3. reservation
4. ghost
5. condemned
6. wander
7. eternity
8. ectoplasm
9. remnants
10. violent
11. vengeful
12. apparition
13. Indian
14. muted
15. tomtom
16. continent
17. equivalent
18. ghoul
19. international
20. ancestor
21. dread
22. cemetery
23. foundation
24. lodge
25. relatives
26. chief
27. Seneca
28. familiar
29. extension
30. crest
31. ditch
32. metaphor
33. cute
34. model
35. spirit
36. weird
37. stranger
38. ignored
39. Cherokee
40. Abenaki
41. development
42. polluted
43. recession
44. depression
45. digressing
46. circle
47. generation
48. Puritan
49. neurotic
50. lantern
51. spooky
52. flickering
53. goofing
54. blond
55. disgust
56. interfere
57. ashamed
58. bridge
59. stagger
60. pale
61. figure
62. shy
63. fool
64. romance
65. moon
66. face
67. skull

**Journal Answers**

*MLA Works Cited.*

Bruchac, Joseph. "Bone Girl." <u>American 24-Karat Gold</u>. 2nd ed. Ed. Yvonne Sisko. New York: Longman, 2007. 104–110.

*Main Character(s).* The narrator and the Bone Girl are the central characters. Certainly, the narrator is the main character. The student may also consider the Bone Girl as main as she is central to the narrator's story and change and she is, after all, the title character.

*Supporting Characters.* The surrounding community on the reservation may be considered supporting. The narrator's wife and nephew and the nephew's friends who have the graveyard adventure are also supporting. The nephew's story is, in fact, a form of foreshadowing. The various ghosts also are supporting here.

*Setting.* This story is set on a present-day reservation. The reservation—and all the qualities the narrator attributes to the reservation—make this location very central to the story. In addition to the key role the reservation plays, another reason this story is placed in *Setting* is because of the important role the Bone Girl's hair plays. It is an important prop because it originally lures the narrator and then becomes a sort of mask to hide the Bone Girl's real identity as a ghost.

*Sequence. Here is an informal outline, but answers will vary.*

   I. Introduction to Indian graveyards.
     A. Close to home.
     B. Native Americans "stay put."

  II. Nephew's graveyard adventure.
     A. Nephew and friends set up trick at the graveyard.
     B. Nephew is tricked by a ghost.

 III. Narrator meets the Bone Girl.
     A. Narrator's life spirals to drinking and available women.
     B. Narrator pursues a young girl who is really a ghost.
     C. Narrator changes his life.

*Plot. With a two-sentence limit, answers will vary.*
A man meets a ghost and changes his wayward life.

*Conflicts.* Human v. supernatural is central here, as ghosts spook both the nephew and then the narrator himself. Human v. himself would apply again to both the nephew and the narrator as their woeful pursuits lead both to encounters with the ghosts. Human v. society may apply to the narrator's unacceptable ways that are changed by the ghostly encounter.

*Significant Quotations.*

a. The student should discuss the narrator's observations on the uniting of present-life and after-life in Native American thought. This thinking is central to setting up the believability of the story.

b. The student should discuss the narrator's observations on the settlement of Native Americans close to ancestral lands. This, also, sets up the story.

c. The student should discuss the graveyard prank played by the nephew and his friends and the ultimate lesson taught by the ghost(s).

d. The student should discuss the narrator's wonton ways and the meeting with the assumed young girl.

e. The student should identify that the narrator meets not a young girl but rather the Bone Girl and that this causes him to change his ways.

## Follow-up Questions. 10 Short Questions

*These are intended for objective assessment and focus on comprehension only, purposely avoiding literary controversy.*

1. b  It is central to understanding the story that the student recognize that the narrator is Native American. This also tests "reservation" and other words from *Context*.

2. a  This tests an important detail. The narrator is married and has taken a wrong turn in life for a married man during the time that he meets the Bone Girl.

3. c  Again, this is central to understanding the story. The narrator clearly tells us that spirits are a part of the Native experience.

4. b  The narrator clearly states and even contrasts the differences between Western and Native spirits. He certainly does not think they are "irrelevant."

5. a  This is the only correct answer here. He certainly believes in spirits and scaring "everyone" offers practice in applying the test-taking technique of avoiding extreme answers.

6. b  The nephew is neither turned into a ghost nor scared by his friends. Rather, it seems that a ghost has now scared him at the graveyard.

7. c  A relevant detail, the narrator tells us that he is writing this story for a writing course. Changing his life seems to "clear his conscience" and he is resentful of "'cute'" Indians.

8. c  The narrator clearly states he has had marital problems. Further, both a

and b apply avoiding extreme answers in test-taking.

9. c    The narrator certainly does *not* think the Bone Girl is a spirit. He *does* think she is a young girl and that she is chilled by the weather. This type of question requires careful reading and offers practice in solving negatively phrased questions.

10. a    The narrator clearly states that he changes his ways as a result of this meeting.

## Follow-up Questions. 5 Significant Quotations

*These are highly focused and are intended for short answer subjective assessment of comprehension only, purposely avoiding literary controversy.*

1. The student should discuss the role of spirits in the narrator's and, by inference, Native American thinking. This closeness is central to making the story believable.

2. The student should discuss the narrator's observations on Native settlement patterns and on the importance of the setting.

3. The student should discuss the nephew's graveyard adventures wherein his trick ends up with a ghost(s) spooking him.

4. The student should discuss the narrator's wonton ways and his pursuit of what turns out to be a ghost.

5. Building on the above answer, the student should discuss the lessons learned from the narrator's meeting with the ghost.

## Follow-up Questions. 2 Comprehension Essay Questions

*These are highly focused and are intended for subjective assessment of comprehension only, purposely avoiding literary controversy or ancillary opinions. Intended to draw upon all facets of the story, 1 and 2 may repeat and/or complement each other.*

1. This asks the student to focus on the setting and the many insights the narrator offers concerning Native Americans, land, and location. Staying close to the land means staying close to the ancestors and spirits that also remain with the land, and this thinking is central to the story.

2. This asks the student to focus on the characters. The narrator and the Bone Girl, of course, are the central story, but the nephew and the graveyard adventures are also part of the story. The student needs to focus on both the

living and the spirits and the lessons learned therein.

## Discussion Questions

*Unlike the Follow-up Questions which are intended to measure comprehension only, thereby avoiding personal opinions and/or literary controversy, these questions are intended to elicit opinions and/or debate. Answers here are only suggestions as the literary discussion may take many forms.*

1. This may elicit varying and often animated responses. The Bone Girl in the story seems to be rather a benevolent character that leads the narrator to reform, but students may bring their own preconceived notions about spirits, ghosts, and the like.

2. Unlike the responses to 1 which have already focused on the ghosts within the story, this asks students now to compare their own feelings and/or experiences with those of the narrator. If 1 focuses on characters then this question focuses on events.

# "AN OCCURRENCE AT OWL CREEK BRIDGE"

Bierce's play with time and place and with fantasy and reality demands close reading on the part of the students. Recognizing time and place is crucial to understanding the story. Although this is a demanding reading, students are generally delighted with themselves and fascinated by the story when they finally figure out all the pieces. Of note, this story has been filmed for television.

**Vocabulary. Words crucial to understanding the story are presented in *Prereading Vocabulary—Context.*** However, all potentially troublesome words are listed here in the order they appear in the text, so that (1) you can easily identify words you may wish to stress and (2) you can locate them easily in the text.

# Vocabulary – "AN OCCURRENCE AT OWL CREEK BRIDGE"

1. occurrence
2. Alabama
3. bound
4. stout
5. slack
6. executioner
7. Federal
8. sergeant
9. deputy
10. sheriff
11. officer
12. uniform
13. captain
14. sentinel
15. vertical
16. hammer
17. forearm
18. erect
19. carriage
20. blockade
21. plank
22. traverse
23. outpost
24. bank
25. acclivity
26. embrasure
27. protrude
28. muzzle
29. cannon
30. fort
31. spectator
32. infantry
33. lieutenant
34. sword
35. adorn
36. statue
37. subordinate
38. dignitary
39. manifestation
40. etiquette
41. deference
42. hang (vb.)
43. apparently
44. civilian
45. habit
46. frock
47. hemp
48. vulgar
49. assassin
50. liberal
51. provision
52. exclude
53. salute
54. pace
55. condemn
56. span
57. former
58. latter
59. tilt
60. commend
61. effective
62. steadfast
63. gaze
64. swirl
65. sluggish
66. brooding
67. mist
68. distract
69. disturbance
70. ignore
71. distinct
72. percussion
73. anvil
74. recurrence
75. toll (vb.)
76. knell
77. apprehension
78. infrequent
79. shriek
80. noose
81. vigorous
82. invader
83. advance
84. doom
85. evolve
86. slave
87. politician
88. original
89. secessionist
90. ardent
91. devoted
92. circumstance
93. imperious
94. gallant
95. disastrous
96. campaign
97. fall
98. chafe
99. restraint
100. distinction
101. perilous
102. consistent
103. assent
104. villainous
105. dictum
106. rustic
107. fetch
108. interfere
109. summarily
110. picket
111. elude
112. accomplish
113. lodge
114. pier
115. ceremonious
116. scout
117. consciousness

118. suffocation
119. keen
120. poignant
121. agony
122. fibre
123. limb
124. ramification
125. inconceivable
126. pulsate
127. intolerable
128. congestion
129. efface
130. luminous
131. fiery
132. arc
133. oscillate
134. pendulum
135. plash
136. strangulation
137. ludicrous
138. inaccessible
139. glimmer
140. reluctance
141. apprise
142. idle
143. feat
144. magnificent
145. endeavor
146. bravo
147. pounce
148. undulation
149. succeed
150. dire
151. pang
152. flutter
153. rack (vb.)
154. wrench (vb.)
155. anguish
156. disobedient
157. emerge
158. convulsive
159. supreme
160. crowning
161. engulf
162. expel
163. preternaturally
164. organic
165. perceive
166. locust
167. prismatic
168. gnat
169. eddy
170. audible
171. pivotal
172. silhouette
173. gesticulate
174. grotesque
175. gigantic
176. monotonous
177. singsong
178. pierce
179. frequent
180. deliberate
181. aspirate
182. chant
183. intonation
184. presage
185. tranquillity
186. volley
187. oscillate
188. descent
189. ramrod
190. socket
191. independent
192. ineffectual
193. current (n.)
194. energetic
195. martinet
196. appalling
197. strangle
198. commotion
199. smitten
200. deflect
201. missile
202. whirl
203. horizontal
204. vortex
205. gyration
206. giddy
207. abrasion
208. gravel
209. resemble
210. fragrance
211. roseate
212. harp
213. enchanting
214. baffle
215. random
216. plunge
217. interminable
218. uncanny
219. revelation
220. fatigue
221. famish
222. dwell
223. habitation
224. terminate
225. diagram
226. perspective
227. rift
228. constellation
229. malign
230. swollen
231. bruise
232. delirium
233. garment
234. veranda
235. ineffable
236. attitude
237. grace
238. stunning
239. blow (n.)

## Journal Answers

*MLA Works Cited.*

Bierce, Ambrose. "An Occurrence at Owl Creek Bridge." <u>American 24-Karat Gold</u>. 2nd ed. Ed. Yvonne Sisko. New York: Longman, 2007. 119–126.

*Main Characters.* Peyton Farquhar is the core of this story as he is tricked by the Federal scout, put on the bridge for execution, dreams of his escape and home-coming, and finally dies.

*Supporting Characters.* First, all the Federal military personnel at the bridge preparing to execute Farquhar are supporting. Second, the Federal scout who probably tricks Farquhar into trying to burn the bridge is supporting. Third, the wife and family he envisions on his return home are supporting.

*Setting.* As noted, recognizing time and place are crucial to understanding this story. In the large picture, it is set during the American Civil War on a railroad bridge somewhere in Alabama and somewhere close to Farquhar's plantation. But in the more specific picture, the location is set on a bridge, then in a stream, then at the plantation gate, and then back on the bridge; the time is set at execu-tion, escape/dream, execution. Students will need to note setting carefully to fol-low the story.

*Sequence. Here is an informal outline, but answers will vary.*

I. Formal execution on the bridge.
   A. Military is formal and silent.
   B. Sergeant and lieutenant are conducting it.
   C. Bridge serves as the gallows.

II. Federal scout's visit.
   A. Confederate soldier visits the plantation and suggests igniting the bridge.
   B. Confederate soldier is really Federal and is tricking Farquhar.

III. Dreams return to the plantation.
   A. Farquhar feels noose and falls to the stream, freeing his hands.
   B. Farquhar sees soldiers shooting and then is swept downstream.
   C. Farquhar is thrown to the bank and struggles through the woods to his home.
   D. Farquhar arrives home to see his approaching wife.

IV. Farquhar is dead from the hanging.

*Plot. With a three-sentence limit, answers will vary.*

A man who is being hanged dreams that he has escaped and returned home, but he is really dead.

*Conflicts.* In this tale of war, this is a human v. society conflict—Farquhar v. the trickery of the Federal military and its scout, Farquhar v. the Federal military and its executioners, a southern gentleman v. the northern army. There is also human v. himself in that Farquhar's pride in wanting to be a man and join the war effort leads him, presumably, to be tricked by the false scout and to try to burn the bridge which leads to his execution.

*Significant Quotations.*

a. The student should discuss the execution by hanging that is going on and the military formality.

b. The student should identify this as Peyton Farquhar and should discuss his gentlemanly life as owner of a plantation ("planter") and not a member of the military ("civilian").

c. This starts the escape dream sequence and the student should discuss that Farquhar first sees himself as escaping the bullets, then making his way through the woods, and then finally making it home when, in fact, he is dead.

d. The student should discuss the scout's trickery. Posing as a Confederate soldier, the Federal scout suggests Farquhar help the war and burn the bridge. It is implied that this sends Farquhar to the hands of the north and he ends up being executed.

e. The student should discuss Farquhar's dreamed homecoming at the plantation and the fact this is a dream or fantasy; Farquhar is dead from the hanging.

*Irony and Foreshadowing. If you have discussed irony and/or foreshadowing, you may want to assign this.*

The irony is the trick played on the reader; while the reader thinks Farquhar is headed home, he is actually at the bridge hung. The foreshadowing hints include the pain in his neck and still manacled hands. Bierce is playing with real and unreal and is playing with the reader all the while.

**Follow-up Questions. 10 Short Questions**
*These are intended for objective assessment and focus on comprehension only, purposely avoiding literary controversy.*

1. a    This is crucial to student understanding. Farquhar is a southern plantation owner and the executing soldiers are northern.

2. c    Farquhar's hanging is the base of the story.

3. a    The scout clearly describes this as a railroad bridge and the open trestles are necessary for the hanging.

4. a    Described as a plantation owner in Alabama, Farquhar is very much the southerner.

5. a    Farquhar's attempt at the bridge is his war effort; he is clearly described as a civilian.

6. b    This is again crucial. It is the northern scout's trick, posing as a Confederate, that sends Farquhar to the bridge.

7. c    We never actually see Farquhar attempt to burn the bridge. This is implied through the scout's suggestion and Farquhar's hanging.

8. b    Farquhar is actually dead. This tests to see if the student has completed and understood the reading.

9. c    The same as 8.

10. c    The same as 8, 9, and 10, all test to see if the student has completed and understood the reading's end.

## Follow-up Questions. 5 Significant Quotations

*These are highly focused and are intended for short answer subjective assessment of comprehension only, purposely avoiding literary controversy.*

1. This describes the hanging setting, and the student should discuss Farquhar and the military prepared to execute him.

2. The student should discuss Farquhar's life as a plantation owner, non-military gentleman.

3. This starts the dream sequence and the student should discuss Farquhar's imagined escape into the stream, away from the bullets, and to the safety of the woods.

4. The student should discuss the story with the scout. A Federal soldier poses as a Confederate and suggests the bridge is ripe for burning. Wanting to help the war effort, presumably Farquhar takes the bait, attempts to burn the bridge, and ends being executed.

5. This is the homecoming and the student should discuss the irreality of the homecoming and reality of the death.

**Follow-up Questions. 2 Comprehension Essay Questions**
*These are highly focused and are intended for subjective assessment of comprehension only, purposely avoiding literary controversy or ancillary opinions. Intended to draw upon all facets of the story, 1 and 2 may repeat and/or complement each other.*

1. The hanging at the bridge is the core of the story. The student should discuss the scout's misleading invitation to burn the bridge, Farquhar's resultant arrest, Farquhar's fantasies, and Farquhar's resultant execution.

2. The student should discuss the differences between the facts of the hanging and the fantasies of escape and homecoming.

**Discussion Questions**
*Unlike the Follow-up Questions which are intended to measure comprehension only, thereby avoiding personal opinions and/or literary controversy, these questions are intended to elicit opinions and/or debate. Answers here are only suggestions as the literary discussion may take many forms.*

1. This focuses students on the events in the story and will bring about lively discussion as they reconstruct all the details that are real and that are fantasy.

2. This focuses the students on the characters and their perceptions, as well as on the events. What Farquhar perceives and what the students perceive are the center here.

## "STRONG TEMPTATIONS—STRATEGIC MOVEMENTS— THE INNOCENTS BEGUILED"

The only selection excerpted from a continuing work, here we have Tom tricking the boys into whitewashing the fence. This is a piece of American lore and a necessary piece of every student's literary lexicon all done in Twain's original language and rich dialogue. This story, as much of Poe's writing, has been presented to students in adaptations (the gist of the story diluted in watered down language, vocabulary, etc.); here, the students can read and study, finally, the real thing. The vocabulary and wonderful dialogue make this demanding reading, but students love the trickery.

**Vocabulary. Words crucial to understanding the story are presented in *Pre-reading Vocabulary—Context.*** However, all potentially troublesome words are listed here in the order they appear in the text, so that (1) you can easily identify words you may wish to stress and (2) you can locate them easily in the text.

# Vocabulary – "STRONG TEMPTATIONS—STRATEGIC MOVEMENTS—THE INNOCENTS BEGUILED"

1. brimming
2. fragrance
3. blossom
4. vegetation
5. repose
6. bucket
7. survey
8. melancholy
9. hollow
10. existence
11. burdened
12. sighing
13. insignificant
14. streak
15. continent
16. discourage
17. pump
18. quarrel
19. skylarking
20. whacks
21. thimble
22. marvel
23. alley
24. waver
25. absorbing
26. bandage
27. wound
28. tingling
29. vigor
30. retiring
31. slipper
32. triumph
33. multiply
34. delicious
35. expedition
36. worldly
37. wealth
38. exchange
39. inspiration
40. magnificent
41. tranquillity
42. hove
43. ridicule
44. dreading
45. anticipations
46. melodious
47. interval
48. personating
49. slacken
50. starboard
51. ponderously
52. pomp
53. circumstance
54. drawing (naut.)
55. laborious
56. stump
57. bight
58. gauge
59. survey
60. ranged
61. druther
62. contemplate
63. suit (vb.)
64. nibbling
65. daintily
66. criticise
67. absorbed
68. reckon
69. core
70. reluctance
71. alacrity
72. sweat
73. barrel
74. dangle
75. slaughter
76. innocent
77. jeer
78. fagged
79. poverty
80. literally
81. jews-harp
82. cannon
83. fragment
84. decanter
85. tadpole
86. dilapidated
87. idle
88. bankrupt
89. covet
90. difficult
91. attain
92. philosopher
93. comprehend
94. oblige
95. construct
96. artificial
97. treadmill
98. amusement
99. wages
100. resign
101. substantial
102. circumstance
103. wend

## Journal Answers

*MLA Works Cited.*

Twain, Mark. "Strong Temptations—Strategic Movements—The Innocents Beguiled." <u>American 24-Karat Gold</u>. 2nd ed. Ed. Yvonne Sisko. New York: Longman, 2007. 135–139.

*Main Characters.* Tom Sawyer is the center of the reading.

*Supporting Characters.* First, there is Aunt Polly who has Tom paint the fence. Then there is Jim off to fetch water, whom Tom first tries to dupe. Then there is the parade of beguiled innocents. Ben comes along intending to tease Tom and ends up as his first victim. Then Billy Fisher, Johnny Miller, and other unnamed boys join in doing Tom's work and adding to his wealth.

*Setting.* Set in Twain's beloved memories of a small riverboat town on the Mississippi, the town is not so crucial as the fence. The fence is more than just a prop; it is central to the story.

*Sequence. Here is an informal outline, but answers will vary.*

I. Tom has to whitewash the fence.
   A. He hates it.
   B. Jim's trip to get water tempts Tom.
   C. Tom tries to lure Jim.

II. Tom has "an inspiration."
   A. Make whitewashing look like fun.
   B. Make whitewashing look so special that others will pay to do it.

III. Tom gets others to whitewash the fence.
   A. Ben comes along to tease Tom and ends up paying an apple core to whitewash.
   B. Billy Fisher pays a kite.
   C. Johnny Miller pays a dead rat and a string.

IV. Tom is rich and has learned to make work look like fun and people will pay to do it.

*Plot. With a two-sentence limit, answers will vary.*
A young boy makes work look like fun and others pay him to do his work.

*Conflicts.* In this joy-filled work, conflict starts with human v. himself and Tom wishing to be anywhere but whitewashing. Human v. human takes place as Tom talks one after another into whitewashing. And Twain's final comment may be human v. society or the assumptions of society, although human v. her/himself applies in Twain's general poke at our willingness to pay for what looks like play (working out at the expensive gym?) v. wanting pay for what looks like work (working out in the backyard weed patch?).

*Significant Quotations.*

   a. The student should explain Tom's whitewashing task and how distasteful it is to him.

   b. This is the moment of Tom's "inspiration" and the student should explain the plan to make work look like fun in order to get others to pay for doing Tom's work.

   c. This starts the specific strategy as Tom responds to Ben's jibes by telling him this is very special work.

   d. This is the moment at which Ben not only takes the paintbrush, but even offers to pay for the honor of painting the fence.

   e. The student should discuss how well Tom's plan has worked; he has gone from poor to rich, in boy wealth, and has had the whitewashing done for him. In discussion, you may want to stress Twain's philosophic observation on this very human condition.

**Follow-up Questions. 10 Short Questions**

*These are intended for objective assessment and focus on comprehension only, purposely avoiding literary controversy.*

   1. a   In order to paint, one can imply it is sunny.

   2. c   Tom clearly hates the whole idea of whitewashing the fence. This is central to the story.

   3. a   Tom clearly states water fetching was a chore, until he sees Jim and it looks like a better option than whitewashing.

   4. c   Tom remembers all the time Jim has spent at the well and even tries to lure Jim into whitewashing in exchange for fetching water.

   5. c   Tom clearly states of all the people he doesn't want to see him at work, Ben is the worst. Ben, meanwhile, shows up taunting Tom with his free time to play riverboat captain.

   6. b   Ben, of course, is not really piloting a riverboat, but rather is playing the part to tease Tom.

   7. a   From Ben's taunts and Tom's response, the student can infer that riverboats are great fun to these boys.

8. c    Part of the ruse is to make whitewashing so special that not everyone can do it so that then, of course, everyone will want to do it.

9. b    The story clearly lists two others—Billy Fisher and Johnny Miller—and Tom's final wealth implies many others.

10. a    This is the core of the story. Yes, Tom tricks them into not only doing, but even paying to do his hated task. "B" and "c" are basically the same answer and cancel out each other.

## Follow-up Questions. 5 Significant Quotations
*These are highly focused and are intended for short answer subjective assessment of comprehension only, purposely avoiding literary controversy.*

1. The student should discuss Tom's task of whitewashing the fence and his abhorring the task.

2. This is the moment that work and fun start to jumble. The student should explain this change and that Tom now considers trading jobs with Jim, because water fetching suddenly looks like fun.

3. The student should explain that Tom has turned the tables and Ben now wants to paint and is willing to pay Tom to do Tom's hated task.

4. This summarizes the ruse (and also checks vocabulary assignment). The student should explain that while Tom looks reluctant to give up the paintbrush, he is, in truth, delighted.

5. This summarizes Twain's tongue-in-cheek philosophical observation. The student should explain that we are willing to donate or even pay for what looks like fun, but if the same endeavor looks like work we want pay. An advanced answer would include a note that the author, and not Tom or another character, is talking here.

## Follow-up Questions. 2 Comprehension Essay Questions
*These are highly focused and are intended for subjective assessment of comprehension only, purposely avoiding literary controversy or ancillary opinions. Intended to draw upon all facets of the story, 1 and 2 may repeat and/or complement each other.*

1. Asking the student to focus on this central prop, the student should discuss the whitewashing chore, the distractions, and Tom's ultimate ruse.

2. This asks the student to focus on the action. The student should discuss

Tom's various tricks (Aunt Polly demands perfection, this is such fun, etc.) and the final results (the fence is done and Tom has amassed his "wealth").

## Discussion Questions

*Unlike the Follow-up Questions which are intended to measure comprehension only, thereby avoiding personal opinions and/or literary controversy, these questions are intended to elicit opinions and/or debate. Answers here are only suggestions as the literary discussion may take many forms.*

1. This will lead to much lively discussion. Opinions will vary depending on students' individual experiences. This focuses students on the events and characters in the story.

2. This truly and personally involves the students. Comparing and contrasting their own trickery with Tom's focuses the students on characters, events, and consequences.

# "THE CASK OF AMONTILLADO"

This marvelously macabre tale is Poe at his best and here the story is presented with all its wonderful, original language. Poe, like Twain, is often presented to middle and high school students in adaptation (the gist of the story framed in watered down vocabulary, dialogue, etc.). Here is the real thing for the students to read and study. The story has been placed in *Setting* because students find this very difficult reading largely due to confusion over the places and things in the story. "Catacombs" is part of the context study for this reason. And students often think Amontillado is a character, which is not altogether incorrect as the wine takes on many player characteristics; an interesting essay test question is: "How is the Amontillado like a character? If it were a character, would be it be male or female? Explain your answer." Students defending it as a male usually explain that it is strong enough to overtake Fortunato. Students defending it as a female usually explain that it seduces Fortunato. And students also have trouble identifying the narrator and Montresor as one and the same. These troubles notwithstanding, students can read through this, perhaps several times, and do finally understand and thoroughly enjoy—*albeit* are outraged by—this wonderfully sinister tale.

**Vocabulary. Words crucial to understanding the story are presented in *Prereading Vocabulary—Context*.** However, all potentially troublesome words are listed here in the order they appear in the text, so that (1) you can easily identify words you may wish to stress and (2) you can locate them easily in the text.

# Vocabulary – "THE CASK OF AMONTILLADO"

1. borne
2. venture
3. insult
4. revenge
5. utterance
6. avenge
7. definitive
8. preclude
9. punish
10. impunity
11. redress
12. retribution
13. doubt
14. wont
15. immolation
16. connoisseur
17. virtuoso
18. enthusiasm
19. imposture
20. gemmary
21. differ
22. vintage
23. supreme
24. carnival
25. encounter
26. accost
27. excessive
28. motley
29. surmount
30. wring
31. pipe
32. bargain
33. whither
34. perceive
35. engagement
36. severe
37. insufferable
38. afflict
39. encrust
40. nitre
41. roquelaire
42. palazzo
43. abscond
44. explicit
45. sconce
46. flambeau
47. suite
48. arch
49. descent
50. catacomb
51. cavern
52. orb
53. distill
54. rheum
55. intoxication
56. precious
57. caution
58. draught
59. mould
60. leer
61. extensive
62. azure
63. serpent
64. rampant
65. cask
66. puncheon
67. intermingle
68. trickle
69. flagon
70. fierce
71. gesticulation
72. grotesque
73. mason
74. trowel
75. jest
76. recoil
77. cloak
78. crypt
79. foul
80. spacious
81. remains (n.)
82. promiscuous
83. interior
84. interval
85. colossal
86. circumscribe
87. granite
88. vain
89. endeavor
90. termination
91. feeble
92. ignoramus
93. extremity
94. niche
95. bewilder
96. fetter
97. staple
98. horizontally
99. pend
100. padlock
101. astound
102. render
103. ejaculate
104. astonish
105. mortar
106. vigorous
107. tier
108. moan

109. obstinate
110. furious
111. vibration
112. shrill
113. hesitate
114. tremble
115. sheath
116. rapier
117. reapproach
118. clamor
119. echo
120. surpass
121. erect
122. noble
123. hearken
124. impatient
125. aperture

## Journal Answers

*MLA Works Cited.*

Poe, Edgar Allan. "The Cask of Amontillado." <u>American 24-Karat Gold</u>. 2nd ed. Ed. Yvonne Sisko. New York: Longman, 2007. 149–155.

*Main Character(s).* The narrator, the meticulously premeditated murderer, the avenger—these are all Montresor. His name is revealed as he and Fortunato pass Montresor's family crest. Fortunato—the duped, the pride-filled, the victim—is the other central character.

*Supporting Characters.* Luchesi is most significant; Montresor uses him to keep luring Fortunato to his pre-appointed tomb. The revelers at the carnival, making noise so Fortunato cannot be heard, and the missing servants, told by Montresor to stay home while he is going out so of course they would go out, may be considered supporting also.

*Setting.* This tale is set in this chapter because place and prop are crucial to the story. The student will need to understand the tunneling nature of the catacombs to make sense of the story (all the bones tend to confuse the student) and to place the murder. And the student will need to recognize that Amontillado, the lure, is a wine; because there is often much confusion over this prop, I usually thoroughly discuss this with students once they have finished the journal but before the test.

*Sequence. Here is an informal outline, but answers will vary.*

I. The insult.
   A. Montresor feels Fortunato has insulted his family.
   B. Montresor plans revenge on Fortunato.

II. The journey down.
   A. Montresor tells his servants he is going out, so that they will go out.
   B. Montresor meets Fortunato at the carnival in the piazza before his house.
   C. Montresor invites Fortunato to sample a pipe of Amontillado.
   D. Montresor and Fortunato descend through the catacombs under Montresor's home to find the wine.
   E. Montresor keeps telling Fortunato they can go back and he will have Luchesi test the wine. This keeps Fortunato going.
   F. They pass Montresor's family crest, and Montresor confirms that his family are masons and reveals a trowel under his cloak.

III. The niche.
   A. Fortunato enters to find the wine.

B. Montresor chains Fortunato.

C. Montresor then bricks in Fortunato, burying him alive.

D. Montresor is avenged and never blamed for the murder.

*Plot. With a three-sentence limit, answers will vary.*

A man avenges an insult to his family by burying the insulter alive.

*Conflicts.* Certainly this is human v. human as Montresor sets out to destroy Fortunato. This is also human v. himself, as Fortunato's prideful connoisseurship leads him to his own destruction.

*Significant Quotations.*

a. The student should discuss Montresor's perception that Fortunato has insulted his family; this sets all the events in motion.

b. The student should discuss Fortunato's fatal pride; this pride leads him to have to sample the Amontillado which leads him to his death.

c. The student should explain that Montresor uses the wine to lure Fortunato to his prearranged tomb. Montresor also uses Luchesi as a lure, in that Fortunato's pride says he has to taste the wine, and not Luchesi, so Fortunato keeps going on to find the Amontillado.

d. The student should explain that Montresor is carrying the murder weapon—the trowel to brick in Fortunato. This is the point at which Montresor has told Fortunato that his family are masons. Both points here are classic examples of Poe's foreshadowing.

e. The student should explain that Fortunato is now being buried alive by Montresor, and that Fortunato dies, buried alive.

*Foreshadowing. This section is added if you have discussed foreshadowing and want students to respond.* Poe often drops all kinds of hints along the way that we all seem to miss on the first reading of his stories and universally end up shocked at the endings. Here, Montresor starts by telling us he is seeking revenge. We start to see through his ruse as he keeps taunting Fortunato with Luchesi. Then, Montresor openly tells us that his family are masons; his family crest says, roughly, "No one can insult us"; and he carries a trowel under his cloak, all the better for burying you, my dear. Poe offers all of these hints of events to come along the way, and yet we all remember our first reading and our astonishment at the live burial. Here, the student can look back and ponder the story for the hints.

## Follow-up Questions. 10 Short Questions

*These are intended for objective assessment and focus on comprehension only, purposely avoiding literary controversy.*

1. b   This is the motivation for the murder; Montresor feels Fortunato has insulted his family and he seeks revenge.
2. a   He is openly jovial and inviting to Fortunato.
3. a   This is fundamental to the story and the reason Montresor can lure Fortunato to his prearranged tomb. Many students confuse the wine with a person.
4. c   The student must infer from Montresor's home or palazzo—with its own catacombs, crest, and wine cellar—that Montresor is quite wealthy and does not work at manual labor.
5. a   Fortunato does not want Luchesi to sample the wine and Montresor successfully uses this jealousy to keep Fortunato descending to the tomb.
6. c   The words, "palazzo," "catacombs," etc. all imply Italy. Further, in the third paragraph Montresor clearly describes both Fortunato and himself as Italians "skillful in the Italian vintages."
7. b   This relates to vocabulary; if the student did the pre-reading work, they will have defined "catacombs" and "crypt" as burial places. This location identification is necessary in understanding the story.
8. b   Again, the role of Luchesi is to tweak Fortunato's pride and to lure him on.
9. a   Most definitely, Montresor has planned well. He has arranged for the servants to leave the house (by telling them they must stay while he will be gone all evening), it is noisy carnival night, and he is carrying a trowel for an obviously well-thought scheme.
10. c   Again, Montresor has clearly stated that he is avenging his family after Fortunato's insult.

## Follow-up Questions. 5 Significant Quotations

*These are highly focused and are intended for short answer subjective assessment of comprehension only, purposely avoiding literary controversy.*

1. The student should explain that Montresor feels Fortunato has insulted his family and sets out to kill him to seek revenge. This statement sets all the plan in motion.

2. The student should discuss Fortunato's pride and that this pride leads him to his death.

3. This is the moment the lure starts. The student should explain that Fortunato will now follow Montresor to find the wine, and to his death.

4. The student should explain that Montresor uses Luchesi as a lure to tweak Fortunato's pride so that he will keep going, ultimately to his tomb.

5. The student should explain that Montresor has buried Fortunato alive ("Against the new masonry I re-erected the old rampart of bones"), and that Fortunato has died in an undiscovered grave while Montresor has never been blamed for the murder ("For half a century no mortal has disturbed them").

## Follow-up Questions. 2 Comprehension Essay Questions

*These are highly focused and are intended for subjective assessment of comprehension only, purposely avoiding literary controversy or ancillary opinions. Intended to draw upon all facets of the story, 1 and 2 may repeat and/or complement each other.*

1. Asking the student to focus on this central prop, the student should discuss the role of the wine as the lure to get Fortunato to his live burial.

2. This makes the student look at the characters carefully. Originally sympathetic to the wronged Montresor and unsympathetic to the arrogant Fortunato, sympathies change as the reader becomes aware of Montresor's diabolical plot.

## Discussion Questions

*Unlike the Follow-up Questions which are intended to measure comprehension only, thereby avoiding personal opinions and/or literary controversy, these questions are intended to elicit opinions and/or debate. Answers here are only suggestions as the literary discussion may take many forms.*

1. This focuses the students on the events and the central characters in the story. The illustration is a marvelous amalgamation of all the pieces in the story and students respond with many insights.

2. Part of the genius of Poe is that he draws us into the insanity. One usually identifies with the narrator as the protagonist, but as this story progresses the arrogant Fortunato becomes more sympathetic and the murderous Montresor becomes more odious. This leads to lively discussion.

# "TO BUILD A FIRE"

In this poignantly brutal tale that is so typically London, instinctive canine is pitted against human learned and arrogantly assumed knowledge, with the dog the victor. This is placed in *Setting* because the frigid surroundings, the avalanching tree, and even the energy of the fire become formidable enemies in setting the action. Students need to recognize the effects of the surroundings as well as the effects of the instinctive as opposed to learned intelligences. Although this story is long and there is much demanding vocabulary, crucial words are presented in *Pre-reading Vocabulary—Context* and students generally read this story well and thoroughly enjoy it.

**Vocabulary. Words crucial to understanding the story are presented in *Pre-reading Vocabulary—Context.*** However, all potentially troublesome words are listed here in the order they appear in the text, so that (1) you can easily identify words you may wish to stress and (2) you can locate them easily in the text.

# Vocabulary – "TO BUILD A FIRE"

1. exceedingly
2. gray
3. aside
4. Yukon
5. trail
6. spruce
7. timberland
8. steep
9. intangible
10. pall
11. subtle
12. gloom
13. absence
14. orb
15. immediately
16. flung
17. undulation
18. jam
19. mysterious
20. tremendous
21. weird
22. impression
23. imagination
24. significance
25. frost
26. meditate
27. frailty
28. creature
29. conjectural
30. immortality
31. universe
32. moccasin
33. precisely
34. speculatively
35. explosive
36. crackle
37. startle
38. spittle
39. claim
40. fork
41. divide
42. possibility
43. protruding
44. handkerchief
45. biscuit
46. sopped
47. plunge
48. faint
49. conclude
50. numb
51. aggressively
52. trot
53. native
54. husky
55. visible
56. temperamental
57. depressed
58. instinct
59. thermometer
60. consciousness
61. brute
62. vague
63. menacing
64. apprehension
65. subdued
66. eagerly
67. unwonted
68. cuddle
69. jowl
70. muzzle
71. crystaled
72. mustache
73. exhale
74. expel
75. amber
76. fragment
77. appendage
78. penalty
79. level
80. boulder
81. calculate
82. drooping
83. discouragement
84. creek
85. furrow
86. monotonously
87. reiterate
88. automatically
89. pang
90. regret
91. keenly
92. observant
93. shied
94. abruptly
95. arctic
96. springs
97. alternate
98. panic
99. delay
100. skirted
101. gingerly
102. gait
103. candied
104. advertised
105. compelled
106. floundered
107. obeyed
108. prompting

109. crypt
110. astonished
111. hastily
112. savagely
113. horizon
114. bulge
115. intervene
116. smash
117. sting
118. thaw
119. threshing
120. reassured
121. lodged
122. seasoned
123. twig
124. outwitted
125. escape
126. singe
127. ancestry
128. inherited
129. abroad
130. whence
131. intimacy
132. caress
133. whiplash
134. communicate
135. welfare
136. yearn
137. whistle
138. proceed
139. imperative
140. tangled
141. deposit
142. portion
143. foundation
144. drowning
145. shred

146. wisp
147. increase
148. squatted
149. entanglement
150. circulation
151. appreciating
152. sensation
153. advice
154. extremities
155. smote
156. recoil
157. willy-nilly
158. ebb
159. recesses
160. rapidity
161. remote
162. conflagration
163. sheath
164. bough
165. freighted
166. agitation
167. imperceptible
168. sufficient
169. capsizing
170. avalanche
171. blotted
172. mantle
173. mate
174. succeed
175. treacherous
176. flotsam
177. methodically
178. wistfulness
179. provider
180. birchbark
181. rustling
182. fumbled

183. surge
184. envy
185. ache
186. excruciating
187. clutch
188. devoting
189. soul
190. obey
191. fiercely
192. manipulation
193. violent
194. devised
195. spasmodically
196. ensued
197. strangling
198. fumes
199. acute
200. endure
201. clumsily
202. jerked
203. sizzling
204. alight
205. cherished
206. perish
207. shiver
208. disrupted
209. nucleus
210. scattered
211. apathetically
212. hunching
213. blizzard
214. carcass
215. suspicious
216. sidled
217. mincingly
218. struggled
219. erect

220. web
221. peremptorily
222. customary
223. allegiance
224. flashed
225. genuine
226. snarled
227. whined
228. struggled
229. throttle
230. plunge
231. halted
232. curiously
233. pricked
234. aroused
235. oppressive
236. poignant
237. strove
238. skim
239. Mercury
240. endurance
241. tottered
242. asserted
243. persisted
244. vision
245. eager
246. security
247. appeasingly
248. pitched
249. conception
250. dignity
251. simile
252. decently
253. glimmerings
254. drowsiness
255. anesthetic
256. mumbled

257. twilight
258. chidden
259. bristle
260. delayed
261. provider

**Journal Answers**

*MLA Works Cited.*

London, Jack. "To Build a Fire." <u>American 24-Karat Gold</u>. 2nd ed. New York: Longman, 2007. 164–177.

*Main Character(s).* The main characters here are the man and the dog, one representing learned and arrogantly assured human knowledge and the other representing instinctive animal wisdom. The very setting also takes on animated qualities as does the elusive nature of the energy of fire.

*Supporting Characters.* Certainly, the old-timer who warns the man about the cold is supporting. The men at the camp, luring the man on, are also supporting. And, as noted with *Main Character(s),* the very setting and the energy of fire support the action.

*Setting.* This story is placed under *Setting* because the lethal cold, the dowsing snow, the spring traps, and the very energy of fire are all players in this story. Specific locations include the trail along the Yukon (and/or this specific tributary), the towns of Sixty Mile where the thermometer is read and Sulphur Creek where the old-timer offers his advice, and Henderson Creek which is the specific artery the man and the dog follow.

*Sequence. Here is an informal outline, but answers will vary.*

  I. Along the Yukon.
    A. It is so bitterly cold, spit freezes in the air.
    B. The man is looking for a logging path for the spring.
    C. The dog instinctively knows it is too cold to be out.

  II. Henderson Creek.
    A. The man has been told and the dog knows to avoid springs that can be lethal traps.
    B. The man forces the dog who gets wet and knows to clean the ice off immediately.
    C. To have lunch, the man builds a fire and then leaves the fire.
    D. The dog knows they should stay by the fire.
    E. The man breaks through into a spring trap and must build another fire.

  III. Building a fire.
    A. Old-timer had warned the man not to travel in this weather alone.
    B. He starts a fire.
    C. It is too close to the spruce, whose branches avalanche and snuff the fire.
    D. The man's fingers are too frozen to separate the matches to start another fire.

E. He finally starts a fire and then clumsily puts it out.
IV. The fire goes out.
   A. The man thinks of killing the dog to warm his hands inside, but the dog knows to stay away.
   B. The man stands and the dog joins him, but the man's frozen hands cannot kill the dog.
   C. The man tries running to warm up, but cannot sustain the running.
   D. The man sits, becomes drowsy, and dies.
   E. The dog smells death and trots off to join the other "fire-providers" at the camp.

*Plot. With a three-sentence limit, answers will vary.*
A man sets out in lethally frigid weather and eventually dies, while the dog he is with knows it is too cold and eventually leaves the dead man to find the camp and warmth.

*Conflicts.* Human v. nature is relevant here on two levels. First and obviously, the man is pitted against the lethal cold and fatal stream bed. Second and more importantly, the learned knowledge of the man is consistently contrasted with the instinctive knowledge of the dog. In this sense, human v. himself is also relevant, as the man's sureness in his man-made lunch and matches prove his downfall. When the spruce branches avalanche snow on the survival fire, London notes, "It [the dowsing avalanche] was his own fault, or, rather, his mistake."

*Significant Quotations.*
   a. The student should explain the severity of the cold and the man's setting out into the cold. Informed with human knowledge by the manmade thermometer, he is too arrogantly ignorant to recognize the message of the cold.
   b. The student should describe the husky and should explain its innate knowledge that, although unaware of a thermometer, he still knows it is too cold to be out.
   c. The student should explain that falling into a hidden spring, covered by thin ice, marks the man's assured downfall. He will have to dry his wet moccasins and clothing with a fire or he will die.
   d. The student should explain that this is the moment before the spruce's branches avalanche the snows that dowse the fire crucial for his survival.
   e. The student should explain that the man cannot get another fire going, that the man tries to lure to dog to kill it and warm his hands, and that, in the end, the man dies from the cold while the dog senses his death and leaves

to find the camp. The student may also explain that the man has not been kind to the dog and that they have not shared a close relationship.

*Foreshadowing.* The very introduction of the setting, with negative words and the spit freezing example all tell us that this is dangerous weather. The old-timer's warnings certainly let us know there is trouble afoot. And the continual contrast of the man's insufficient learned knowledge with the dog's innate knowledge consistently suggest the man will not survive.

## Follow-up Questions. 10 Short Questions

*These are intended for objective assessment and focus on comprehension only, purposely avoiding literary controversy.*

1. b    Although it would be nice if the student actually got out a map, "Yukon" is a context word with reference to Alaska. Further, the very severity of the weather suggests "northern." "Eastern America" does not imply this kind of cold and, of course, "Africa" implies heat.

2. c    Indicating understanding, it is because the man stays by the water that he puts himself and the dog at great risk of the spring traps.

3. a    London tells us at the very beginning that the man is looking for logging routes for use in the spring.

4. b    Again indicating understanding, we are continually told that the dog knows it is too cold to be out.

5. b    Once the first fire is built, the dog does not understand and does not want to leave the fire, knowing it should be curled up by its warmth.

6. a    Again indicating understanding, the theme of the story is the dog's innate wisdom v. the man's learned but unproductive knowledge; the dog *knows* it is too cold to be out.

7. c    The old-timer has told him it was too cold to be out and the old-timer has told him to have a partner. The man heeds neither advice and, at one point, refers to the old-timer's advice as "womanly"—until he starts dying.

8. a    Again indicating understanding, it is because the fire is too close to the spruce that, when the wood-gathering movements cause the avalanche, the snow is close enough to put out the fire. Had the fire been away from the avalanching branches, the fire might have survived.

9. c    The man attempts to call the dog to kill him and then attempts again but is too frozen to function. The dog does not heed the first call and escapes

the attempt. The man wants to kill the dog to warm his hands inside the carcass, but he is unsuccessful and does not kill the dog.

10. b    The man dies from the cold and the dog sets off to return to camp. Both 9 and 10 test if the student has successfully completed the story.

## Follow-up Questions. 5 Significant Quotations

*These are highly focused and are intended for short answer subjective assessment of comprehension only, purposely avoiding literary controversy.*

1. The student should introduce the man and explain that, while the man has human knowledge from the thermometer and the old-timer, he heeds neither and arrogantly sets out to his own demise.

2. The student should describe the husky and explain its wisdom and instinctive knowledge that it is too cold to be out traveling.

3. The student should explain that this is the moment the man gets his moccasins and clothes wet and that this, basically, marks the man's demise. The student should explain that he must build a fire to survive.

4. The student should explain that this moment seals the man's doom. Because he has unwisely built so close to the tree, the fire is extinguished after the branches avalanche due to the movement of firewood under the tree. The student should explain that the man is unable to build another fire because he is too frozen to manipulate the man-made but now useless matches and, from this point on, he is on a direct line to dying.

5. The student should explain that the man has died from the cold and that the dog will now follow its own instinctive map to get back to humans, the "fire-providers" and "food-providers."

## Follow-up Questions. 2 Comprehension Essay Questions

*These are highly focused and are intended for subjective assessment of comprehension only, purposely avoiding literary controversy and/or ancillary opinions. Intended to draw upon all facets of the story, 1 and 2 may repeat and/or complement each other.*

1. The failure of the fire is central to the story. The student should discuss the utter cold, the warnings, the dog's instincts, and the man's combined arrogance and ignorance that lead him to freeze to death in the absence of the fire he cannot build.

2. Like 1, the student should discuss the dog's innate knowledge that tells him

it is too cold to be out, that tells him to walk away from the water, that tells him to shun the man, etc. The student should contrast this with the man's combined arrogance and ignorance that ultimately lead him to his death.

## Discussion Questions

*Unlike the Follow-up Questions which are intended to measure comprehension only, thereby avoiding personal opinions and/or literary controversy, these questions are intended to elicit opinions and/or debate. Answers here are only suggestions as the literary discussion may take many forms.*

1. This focuses the students on the very conflict in the story, as the illustration depicts the moment when the man approaches the dog to kill him and seek warmth in his body. This story usually evokes strong feelings and the illustration presents not only a key moment, for the man is condemned to die after this last failed attempt, but also leads the students to reflect on the events leading up to this moment.

2. This focuses the students on the characters themselves. Opinions may vary greatly here. While the dog is London's intended protagonist, students may vary in their reactions to the characters and to humankind's arrogance in and of itself.

# CHAPTER THREE

## *PLOT and Foreshadowing*

## "SALVATION"

This is the classic and poignant tale of the little boy who is so lost—and ultimately so disillusioned—at trying to understand and to please others. Students enjoy this short yet rich tale that is readable to all students.

**Vocabulary. Words crucial to understanding the story are presented in *Prereading Vocabulary—Context*.** However, all potentially troublesome words are listed here in the order they appear in the text, so that (1) you can easily identify words you may wish to stress and (2) you can locate them easily in the text.

# Vocabulary – "SALVATION"

1. sin
2. revival
3. preaching
4. praying
5. Christ
6. bound
7. lamb
8. escort
9. mourner
10. bench
11. soul
12. sermon
13. dire
14. hell
15. knelt
16. braided
17. rocked
18. altar
19. deacon
20. whisper
21. damn
22. alone
23. swirled
24. congregation
25. mighty
26. wail
27. moan
28. serenely
29. ashamed
30. platform
31. knickerbockered
32. grinning
33. vain
34. lying
35. temple
36. sea
37. rejoicing
38. swept
39. leaped
40. minister
41. hushed
42. silence
43. punctuated
44. ecstatic
45. amen
46. buried
47. quilt
48. Holy Ghost
49. Jesus
50. lied
51. deceived

**Journal Answers**

*MLA Works Cited.*

Hughes, Langton. "Salvation." <u>American 24-Karat Gold</u>. 2nd ed. Ed. Yvonne
 Sisko. New York: Longman, 2007. 187–189.

*Main Character(s).* The narrator is the central character in this story. He is the
little boy who is trying so hard to please and to understand this adult world.

*Supporting Characters.* For a very short story, there are plenty of characters
here, and the student may find these characters interchangeable as main or supporting characters. God, of course, and Christ coming are also central characters.
Aunt Reed initiates and reinforces the action. The girls, who receive God first;
Westley, who lies his way through it first; and the surrounding congregation are
all relevant players here.

*Setting.* The setting at the revival meeting is essential to the story dynamics.
While this could take place at a church anywhere, the intensity of the rite is necessary to the action.

*Sequence. Here is an informal outline, but answers will vary.*

 I. The narrator goes to the revival.
 A. Aunt Reed and the congregation expect him to see the Lord.
 B. The girls see the Lord first.

 II. The narrator and God.
 A. The narrator and Westley don't see the Lord.
 B. Westley lies.
 C. The narrator lies.

 III. The narrator and his lies.
 A. The narrator feels guilty about lying.
 B. The narrator becomes disillusioned and loses faith.

*Plot. With a two-sentence limit, answers will vary.*
A boy is expected to see God in front of many people, and suffers personal consequences from lying his way through the experience.

*Conflicts.* Human v. supernatural is central here as the narrator and God seem to
be at odds with each other. Human v. society certainly applies to the conflict the
narrator feels between himself and the rest of the congregation. Further, lying is
at odds with general societal and specific Ten Commandments dictates. Human
v. himself applies to both the narrator and Westley as they lie their ways out of
this difficult situation.

*Significant Quotations.*

a. This sets the stage and the student should describe the location.

b. This sets the action and the student should discuss the expectations that are placed on the narrator to see God.

c. This establishes the tension and the student should discuss the pressure that is placed on the children to see God.

d. The student should discuss the girls first seeing God and then Westley's lie, that then ultimately sets up the narrator's lie.

e. The student should discuss the narrator's lie and his resultant guilt and/or resentment and/or disillusionment.

**Follow-up Questions. 10 Short Questions**

*These are intended for objective assessment and focus on comprehension only, purposely avoiding literary controversy.*

1. c   In this very personal narrative that is as much essay as it is story, the student should be able to infer that the narrator and the author are probably one and the same. If the author were a relative or a different person, he probably would not have used first-person narration.

2. a   This is central to understanding the story and reinforces the *Context* vocabulary. The narrator is there to see God and that is a religious experience.

3. c   The student needs to infer that the narrator lives with Aunt Reed. There is, of course, nothing to imply that he lives with Westley and there is no mention of his parents. Further, the biography notes Hughes' residence with his grandmother, another extended relative.

4. b   Change is crucial here. "Sinner" implies needing fixing, and here accepting God is the crux of the story.

5. b   While there is talk of hearing and feeling, he is instructed that he must see God.

6. a   An important detail that sets up the tension, the girls see God first, which leads to pressure on Westley and the narrator to move along and also see God.

7. a   These are the young, the new initiates—the children who are to see God and be saved.

8. b   This is all lively with praying and jubilation. Further, both "a" and "c" cancel each other out in applying process-of-elimination in testing.

9. c  This is a crucial detail. Westley does not see God but he lies, thereby setting up the narrator.

10. c  This is also crucial and fundamental to the story. The narrator does not see God but says he does and suffers general disillusionment from the whole experience.

## Follow-up Questions. 5 Significant Quotations

*These are highly focused and are intended for short answer subjective assessment of comprehension only, purposely avoiding literary controversy.*

1. The student should describe the revival setting and the youthful narrator's place in the setting.

2. The student should describe Aunt Reed and the expectations that are placed on the narrator.

3. The student should describe the tension that is building and Westley's lie to get himself out of this difficult situation, the lie that sets up the narrator's lie.

4. The student should identify this as the moment of climax and should explain that the narrator has now also decided to lie his way out of this difficult situation.

5. The student should discuss the narrator's lie and the guilt and disillusionment that result from this lie.

## Follow-up Questions. 2 Comprehension Essay Questions

*These are highly focused and are intended for subjective assessment of comprehension only, purposely avoiding literary controversy or ancillary opinions. Intended to draw upon all facets of the story, 1 and 2 may repeat and/or complement each other.*

1. This focuses the student on the central character and events of the story.

2. This focuses the student on the setting and the related characters that swirl around the narrator.

## Discussion Questions

*Unlike the Follow-up Questions which are intended to measure comprehension only, thereby avoiding personal opinions and/or literary controversy, these questions are intended to elicit opinions and/or debate. Answers here are only suggestions as the literary discussion may take many forms.*

1. This draws on each student's own experiences and relates those experiences to the characters and the events in the story. This discussion may lead in many directions depending on the experiences the students bring to this discussion.

2. There are several here that the students may note. There is the unholy pressure of becoming holy, the adults that one may assume are veteran sinners but who claim to have seen God and the innocent children who cannot see God, and the ultimate lie told in God's presence about God. Students may need some prompting with ironies.

## "THE LADY OR THE TIGER?"

In Stockton's enduring tale, the reader is left hanging and must supply her/his own ending. This is placed in *Plot* because this story makes the student very aware of climax and dénouement, which is missing. The language is formal and there is much demanding vocabulary, but students enjoy this story and sustain reading out of sheer interest. Further, words crucial to understanding the story are presented in *Pre-reading Vocabulary—Context.*

**Vocabulary. Words crucial to understanding the story are presented in *Pre-reading Vocabulary—Context.*** However, all potentially troublesome words are listed in the order they appear in the text, so that (1) you can easily identify words you may wish to stress and (2) you can locate them easily in the text.

# Vocabulary – "THE LADY OR THE TIGER?"

1. barbaric
2. progressive
3. florid
4. trammel
5. exuberant
6. fancy
7. authority
8. commune
9. domestic
10. political
11. bland
12. genial
13. orb
14. crooked
15. semified
16. exhibition
17. valor
18. cultured (adj.)
19. assert
20. rhapsody
21. gladiator
22. inevitable
23. amphitheater
24. gallery
25. mysterious
26. vault
27. punish
28. virtue
29. decree
30. impartial
31. accuse
32. sufficient
33. fate
34. emanate
35. barleycorn
36. tradition
37. allegiance
38. ingrafted
39. assemble
40. court
41. throne
42. privilege
43. directly
44. guidance
45. influence
46. procure
47. doleful
48. clang
49. wail
50. mourner
51. audience
52. wend
53. dire
54. suitable
55. majesty
56. affection
57. subordinate
58. interfere
59. scheme
60. retribution
61. tread
62. epithalamic
63. solemnize
64. peal
65. precede
66. strew
67. devour
68. tribunal
69. judgment
70. institution
71. trial
72. slaughter
73. hilarious
74. occasion
75. masses
76. community
77. daughter
78. soul
79. fervent
80. imperious
81. courtier
82. station
83. conventional
84. royal
85. surpass
86. ardor
87. exceed
88. hesitate
89. waver
90. premises
91. slight
92. novel
93. startling
94. savage
95. rank
96. survey (vb.)
97. competent
98. destiny
99. deed
100. deny
101. dispose
102. aesthetic
103. throng
104. portal
105. admiration
106. anxiety
107. moiety
108. fervid
109. emerge
110. blushing
111. radiant

112. damsel
113. aspire
114. perceive
115. dare
116. transmit
117. ancestor
118. tremble
119. crouch
120. assure
121. flash
122. parapet
123. rapid
124. devious
125. maze
126. passion
127. despair
128. jealousy
129. horror
130. grievous
131. revery
132. gnash
133. rapturous
134. agony
135. kindle
136. multitude
137. tremendous
138. shriek
139. indicate
140. anguish
141. deliberation
142. presume

## Journal Answers

*MLA Works Cited.*

Stockton, Frank. "The Lady or the Tiger?" <u>American 24-Karat Gold</u>. 2nd ed. Ed. Yvonne Sisko. New York: Longman, 2007. 198–203.

*Main Character(s).* The princess and the courtier are central to this story. It is their love that initiates the courtier's trial. Students may arguably include the king who set up the amphitheatre justice and the tiger whose presence is so vital to the story's tension.

*Supporting Characters.* If the king and the tiger are not discussed as main characters, they certainly belong in supporting characters. The damsel, the object of the princess' jealousy and the chosen one for the courtier, is certainly an essential dynamic also, because the princess' jealousy of her leaves us in doubt as to the princess' decision. The attending crowds, cheering on this violent justice, also play a role here, as do the jailers who tell the princess which door is which. Of note, all criminals are assumed to be male in this story's world.

*Setting.* Although set in a kingdom in a time long past, it is interesting to discuss the whole concept of totalitarian state and life-and-death authority with American students. Although Stockton tells us this is an ancient time, it is perhaps worthy to remind students that there are many places in the world today where totalitarianism exists. Further, the very dynamic of the amphitheatre and its "benevolent" justice gives the arena character-like traits.

*Sequence. Here is an informal outline, but answers will vary.*

I. The king builds an arena/amphitheatre.
   A. The purpose is to resolve innocence and guilt.
   B. If one chooses one door, the tiger comes out to eat him and he is assumed guilty.
   C. If one chooses the other door, the fair maiden comes out to marry him and he is assumed to be innocent.

II. The princess and courtier fall in love.
   A. He is beneath her in "station."
   B. The king sends him to prison to await trial in the amphitheatre.
   C. The princess is jealous of the damsel chosen for him.

III. The trial.
   A. The princess finds out which door is which.
   B. The courtier looks to the princess.
   C. She nods to the right door.

IV. The decision.
   A. Does the princess send the courtier to his death or marriage?
   B. Does the courtier heed the princess or choose the other door?

*Plot. With a three-sentence limit, answers will vary.*
A courtier and princess fall in love and he turns to her for life and/or death.

*Conflicts.* The courtier demonstrates human v. society in his conflict with the societally imposed arena justice system. The courtier demonstrates human v. human, also, as he is in conflict with the justice system that has been instituted, after all, by the king. The courtier also demonstrates human v. nature in his potential bout with the tiger. The princess demonstrates human v. herself in the tension that arises from her jealousy vying with her compassion. Her very conflict is crucial to the tension and, of course, the unresolved end.

*Significant Quotations.*

   a. This refers to the amphitheatre and the student should explain both the structure and the purpose of the structure.

   b. This refers to the two doors of choice and the student should discuss the system of justice and that one door contains a tiger, signifying horrible death and assumed guilt, while the other contains a fair maiden, implying happy life and assumed innocence. The student should also mention that the door is the criminal's free choice.

   c. This describes the courtier and the student should discuss his love for the princess and the forbidden nature of this love. Although he is brave and handsome, he is below the princess and not allowed to marry her and, therefore, ends up being sent to trial by her father, the king.

   d. This describes the moment the princess observed the damsel interacting with the courtier. The student should explain the moment and explain that this sets up the princess' jealousy over this maiden who could marry her courtier if he picks her door.

   e. This is the moment of climax that is unresolved. The student should explain that this is the point the story leaves the reader outraged in that the story does not tell us if the courtier lives or dies.


**Follow-up Questions. 10 Short Questions**
*These are intended for objective assessment and focus on comprehension only, purposely avoiding literary controversy.*

1. a   This tests understanding "barbaric" and the nature of the king. He is, obviously, not kind and his frivolous system is certainly not fair. However, we are clearly told he is "barbaric," and "brutal" best approximates "barbaric."

2. c   Although he may be barbaric, he feels and gives a whole rationale for the fairness of the arena justice system.

3. c   The princess is clearly described as passionate. Further, it is this very passion that makes the reader unsure of her final decision.

4. b   The courtier is not royal, unworthy of the princess and unacceptable according to the king, and ends up in this trial because he is not royal. This tests vocabulary as well as a fundamental understanding of the story.

5. c   He is so outraged that he commits the courtier to possible death in the arena.

6. b   Again, retesting a major point, the king is outraged that his daughter is associating with a common man. If a student misses 4, 5, and/or 6, s/he has missed a major factor in the story. It is the king's very distaste that lands the courtier in the arena.

7. a   We are clearly told that the princess bribes the guards to find out which door is which. "B" and "c" are basically the same, erroneous answer.

8. b   Again, we are clearly told the princess bribes the guards.

9. a   Crucial to the tension, we are told of the princess' jealousy over the maiden which, we assume, will affect her decision in advising the courtier.

10. b   Also crucial to the tension, the princess loves the courtier and does not want him dead. If she does not care if he is dead or alive, we can safely assume she tosses him to the tiger and there is no unsureness. It is because she cannot bear to see him torn apart that we are unsure of her decision. "A" and "c" are basically the same answer. Questions 9 and 10 review the tension.

## Follow-up Questions. 5 Significant Quotations

*These are highly focused and are intended for short answer subjective assessment of comprehension only, purposely avoiding literary controversy.*

1. The student should explain the structure of the arena and the arena justice system.

2. The student should explain the role of the doors in the justice system. Here, the student should explain that "came out of it a hungry tiger" means the person has chosen the door with the tiger which means a horrible death and sig-

nifies guilt. "But if the accused opened the other door" means the person has chosen a lovely maiden that he will marry and he is presumed innocent.

3. "This royal maiden" refers to the princess and "her lover" refers to the courtier. The student should explain that the princess loves a lover beneath her and that he ends up being sent to the arena by her father, the king.

4. This describes the damsel and summarizes the princess' hate for her. The student should explain the damsel's role in complicating the princess' decision.

5. The student should explain the courtier's trust in the princess and the great question the story leaves us with: does the princess signal life with the damsel or death with the tiger?

## Follow-up Questions. 2 Comprehension Essay Questions

*These are highly focused and are intended for subjective assessment of comprehension only, purposely avoiding literary controversy or ancillary opinions. Intended to draw upon all facets of the story, 1 and 2 may repeat and/or complement each other.*

1. The student should describe the amphitheater and the two-door justice system. The student should then relate the forbidden interest between the princess and the unworthy courtier. The student should include the princess' jealousy of the maiden and the princess' ultimate decision process.

2. The student should discuss the princess' interest in the unworthy courtier that ultimately leads him to the amphitheater. The student should discuss the princess' jealousy of the very maiden that the courtier will be offered. The student should discuss the princess' bribe to learn what door has what and the student should discuss the final dilemma, heightened by the princess' jealousy of the maiden.

## Discussion Questions

*Unlike the Follow-up Questions which are intended to measure comprehension only, thereby avoiding personal opinions and/or literary controversy, these questions are intended to elicit opinions and/or debate. Answers here are only suggestions as the literary discussion may take many forms.*

1. This generally brings about a more global discussion. Students must reflect not only on the events in the story, but also on the events in their own lives

that demonstrate the castes in our society, in their families, communities, and so forth.

2. This focuses the students on the characters and on their own reactions to the characters. Some will feel more sympathy for one character than another and this leads to very lively discussion.

## "NO NAME WOMAN"

This heart-wrenching tale carries student interest throughout the reading. This is really a narrative essay, but it is included in this collection because the story is so very strong and because the narrator's commentary is necessary to help explain the dynamics of the narrative. It is included in *Plot* because the events are, very simply, the story. Further, the Journal includes a section on *Foreshadowing*; while there is not so much foreshadowing as there is a mingling of past narrative and present commentary, this section is intended to get the student thinking about the mixture of time.

**Vocabulary. Words crucial to understanding the story are presented in *Prereading Vocabulary—Context.*** However, all potentially troublesome words are listed here in the order they appear in the text, so that (1) you can easily identify words you may wish to stress and (2) you can locate them easily in the text.

# Vocabulary – "NO NAME WOMAN"

1. well
2. village
3. celebrated
4. responsibly
5. contracts
6. decks
7. stowaway
8. protruding
9. melon
10. pregnant
11. raided
12. saw (n.)
13. zigzag
14. lantern
15. bound
16. mask
17. slaughtering
18. stock
19. flared
20. panes
21. smeared
22. splattering
23. arc
24. ancestors
25. wings
26. enclose
27. comb
28. grinding
29. loom
30. weaving
31. acrid
32. torrent
33. sobbed
34. scolded
35. preserves
36. pigsty
37. plugging

38. denies
39. menstruate
40. humiliate
41. establish
42. realities
43. emigrant
44. generations
45. reassert
46. brute
47. survival
48. diverting
49. curse
50. crooked
51. offspring
52. similar
53. sojourners
54. poverty
55. insanities
56. flashy
57. ordinary
58. necessity
59. riverbank
60. frivolous
61. carnival
62. guilt
63. adultery
64. extravagance
65. embryos
66. delicacies
67. gravel
68. gizzard
69. engender
70. prodigal
71. starvation
72. romantic
73. commanded
74. evil

75. encountered
76. fuel
77. stranger
78. adjoining
79. terrified
80. obeyed
81. tractably
82. proxy
83. advantage
84. envision
85. separated
86. rape
87. hazarded
88. permeated
89. outcast
90. commensal
91. precious
92. samurai
93. geisha
94. averted
95. glowering
96. offender
97. synonym
98. mortgaged
99. stoned
100. mysterious
101. disgrace
102. deflect
103. avenger
104. dispensed
105. barbarians
106. fumble
107. detection
108. maintain
109. rare
110. urge
111. delineated

112. preservation
113. forerunner
114. persisted
115. enormities
116. forbidden
117. torso
118. vanished
119. pigtail
120. erase
121. subtle
122. rollicking
123. sustain
124. reputation
125. eccentricity
126. braided
127. individuality
128. bob
129. bun
130. contrived
131. wisps
132. strand
133. captive
134. depilatory
135. bound
136. freckle
137. almanac
138. predestined
139. peroxide
140. feasting
141. hexes
142. whorls
143. goddesses
144. warriors
145. marvelous
146. burden
147. imminent
148. restraining

149. curiosity
150. startled
151. spoiled
152. gazing
153. affection
154. lavished
155. bayoneted
156. doted
157. efface
158. miens
159. ideal
160. blur
161. immigrant
162. unmodulated
163. erect
164. inaudible
165. communication
166. whisper
167. preoccupied
168. singularity
169. accuse
170. punished
171. inseminator
172. intercourse
173. kinsmen
174. titles
175. neutralized
176. circumvent
177. incest
178. surnames
179. mannerisms
180. atavism
181. benevolence
182. attraction
183. selective
184. direction
185. magnitude

186. dignified
187. eludes
188. societies
189. adult
190. dowries
191. siblings
192. structure
193. spirits
194. shimmered
195. equilibrium
196. maelstrom
197. misallying
198. embodied
199. betrayed
200. severe
201. greedy
202. plagues
203. bandit
204. graduated
205. talisman
206. descent
207. infidelity
208. consequences
209. disguise
210. circumference
211. inexorable
212. culpability
213. wrest
214. seize
215. gall
216. convulsed
217. complexity
218. companion
219. eternal
220. agoraphobia
221. flayed
222. spasmodically

223. alternately
224. obliterated
225. gambling
226. massaging
227. jealous
228. gods
229. spasms
230. tribal
231. foreign
232. expelled
233. precisely
234. squirmed
235. thrashed
236. clenched
237. wound
238. abandon
239. frail
240. participate
241. chase
242. reverse
243. worship
244. inflicted
245. deliberately
246. descendants
247. decoy
248. unharassed
249. eternity
250. essences
251. incense
252. attempt
253. replicas
254. haunts
255. devote
256. origamied
257. spite

258. suicide
259. bloated
260. substitute

**Journal Answers**

*MLA Works Cited.*

Hong Kingston, Maxine. "No Name Woman." <u>American 24-Karat Gold</u>. 2nd ed. Ed. Yvonne Sisko. New York: Longman, 2007. 212–222.

*Main Character(s).* The two main characters are the aunt (the No Name Woman) and the narrator (Hong Kingston). The aunt is a woman living in China who becomes pregnant and ends up killing herself and her newborn in the family well. The narrator is a Chinese American writer who seems to seek peace in writing this reflective narrative essay. The baby is also central, although the student may consider the brief appearance of the newborn supporting. However, it is the baby that fuels the actions.

*Supporting Characters.* If the baby is not discussed as a main character, she (Hong Kingston implies that had it been a boy, it might still be alive) certainly should be discussed as supporting. Hong Kingston's mother, who tells her the story, and father, whose family witnessed the death, are certainly supporting. The man who impregnated the aunt, and whose identity is never revealed save that he is not the aunt's husband who is in America, is certainly supporting. In fact, a good deal of Hong Kingston's analysis deals with whom he might be. The villagers who come to deface the home are also supporting. The death is largely a result of their rabid ostracism.

*Setting.* Set in a small village in China among poor people during a past generation, the student might comment that this could possibly take place in any small town. The severe ostracism and the cultural taboo, however, may be somewhat unique to a poor and/or tribal matrix.

*Sequence. Here is an informal outline, but answers will vary.*

I. Aunt's pregnancy.
   A. The aunt is returned to her own family's home, and does not stay with her husband's family when he goes to America, which is considered odd.
   B. The aunt becomes pregnant by someone other than her husband, but by someone who is not a stranger in this small village.
   C. The villagers raid the home to destroy the spirits.

II. Hong Kingston questions why the aunt is pregnant.
   A. This could be someone the aunt knew who demanded and/or raped her.
   B. This could be someone the aunt sought to lure.
   C. The aunt may have been a doted-upon daughter who attracted him.

III. The death.

A. The aunt keeps the father a secret.
B. The aunt starts labor in the fields.
C. The aunt delivers in the pigsty to trick the spirits.
D. The aunt suckles the newborn and comes to care for it.
E. The aunt drowns herself and the baby in the family well.

IV. Aftermath.
A. The aunt is erased from the family, hence "No Name Woman."
B. Hong Kingston is easing her own discomfort and/or fending off the drowning spirit that seeks to pull down a substitute.

*Plot. With a three-sentence limit, answers will vary.*
A woman becomes pregnant and is ostracized and ultimately kills herself and her newborn by drowning in the family well.

*Conflicts.* Human v. society is relevant in the cultural ostracism that leads to the deaths. Human v. human is relevant in the aunt's relationship with the father. Hong Kingston makes it clear that this is someone from the village whom the aunt does not reveal and could well be someone who forced the aunt and who certainly does not take responsibility for the pregnancy. Human v. herself may apply to both the aunt and Hong Kingston. Crushed by the ostracism, the aunt kills herself while Hong Kingston seems to be working out ghosts in this essay.

*Significant Quotations.*

a. The student should explain this describes the aunt's plight. She is pregnant by someone other than her husband who is in America and this is not acceptable.
b. The student should explain that, in violent disapproval, the village people come to the house and destroy much. This is overt ostracism.
c. The student should explain that Hong Kingston analyzes who the father may be. The student should note that Hong Kingston makes it clear that the father is no stranger, as everyone knows everyone in this small village, and that he may even have been one of those to ransack the house. She implies he is not much of a person.
d. The student should explain that the aunt never reveals the father's name. The student should explain this leads Hong Kingston to offer much speculation (force, rape, allurement, etc.).
e. The student should explain that the aunt delivers the baby by herself in the pigsty (to ward off spirits) and drowns herself and the newborn. The student should comment on this very statement which states that the female is

unwanted and implies that a male newborn might have saved both their lives.

*Foreshadowing*. We are told at the very beginning that the aunt had killed herself in the family well. We are told about the pregnancy and the villagers' violent reaction. Hong Kingston explains the village's poverty and then speculates on the father. In her speculations, it can be implied that she is sympathetic to the aunt and that the baby's father is an inferior character. Perhaps nothing prepares us for the ultimate infanticide, but the suicide is clearly stated and then analyzed.

## Follow-up Questions. 10 Short Questions
*These are intended for objective assessment and focus on comprehension only, purposely avoiding literary controversy.*

1. c   Hong Kingston clearly notes that her parents lived in China and now live in America so, therefore, she lives in America. "Japan" might indicate inaccurate reading and/or thinking.

2. a   Her mother tells of the men going to America from China. In fact, the aunt's husband was with Hong Kingston's father in America after the time of the impregnation. Her father has clearly lived in both America and China.

3. b   Indicating understanding, this terrible tragedy occurs because the aunt is not married to the baby's father. She certainly knows the father because we are told this is a small village and a stranger would be noticed.

4. a   They ransack the house and bring severe unpleasantness, but no one personally attacks or kills the aunt; she commits suicide at her own hand.

5. a   Hong Kingston clearly tells us that everyone knows everyone in this small town.

6. b   Hong Kingston strongly implies that the aunt may have been forced, but no reason for the tryst is clearly stated.

7. b   Again, Hong Kingston discusses this but there is no sure information.

8. b   The aunt seems to care vitally about the villagers' concern and commits suicide and infanticide in the face of brutal ostracism.

9. c   The aunt "cares" on two levels. First, she takes care of the baby by nursing it after birth. Second, she comes to care about the baby and "its preciousness" and does not "Turn its face into the mud," but rather Hong Kingston states, "Mothers who love their children take them along," rather than abandon them or leave them to ravages.

10. c  She is not killed and she does not simply commit suicide herself. She kills both herself and her newborn, so "c" is the best answer and checks if the student has accurately read all choices.

## Follow-up Questions. 5 Significant Quotations
*These are highly focused and are intended for short answer subjective assessment of comprehension only, purposely avoiding literary controversy.*

1. The student should discuss the aunt's suicide, which starts the story. The aunt commits suicide in the well, a context word, after giving birth to an illegitimate child.

2. The student should discuss the villagers' violent disapproval of the forbidden pregnancy, which they look on as a betrayal in this impoverished village.

3. The student should explain that the aunt knew the baby's father before the impregnation because everyone knows everyone in this small village. In a more complete answer, the student might discuss Hong Kingston's theories of force or rape, enticement, or attraction.

4. The student should discuss that the aunt never reveals the baby's father's name. If the student has not discussed impregnation theories in 3, s/he might do so here.

5. The student should explain that these are the few living moments of the newborn. The student should explain that the aunt loves this little one and that she drowns herself and the baby with her.

## Follow-up Questions. 2 Comprehension Essay Questions
*These are highly focused and are intended for subjective assessment of comprehension only, purposely avoiding literary controversy or ancillary opinions. Intended to draw upon all facets of the story, 1 and 2 may repeat and/or complement each other.*

1. The student should relate the story of the No Name Woman. Details should include: the husband's immigration to America; the untimely pregnancy, by a man of the town; the town's ostracism; and the wrenching suicide and infanticide.

2. The student should discuss the gender discrimination here. The woman is solely responsible for the pregnancy, while the father can safely be assumed to be a man in the village whose identity the No Name Woman seems to be

obligated to protect; he is free of onus while she will ultimately kill herself and the baby out of ostracism and shame. The student should discuss the overt ostracism of the villagers toward the No Name Woman. And the student should discuss the final comment that, had the baby been a boy, he might have been salvageable, but a girl is considered worth little.

## Discussion Questions

*Unlike the Follow-up Questions which are intended to measure comprehension only, thereby avoiding personal opinions and/or literary controversy, these questions are intended to elicit opinions and/or debate. Answers here are only suggestions as the literary discussion may take many forms.*

1. This is a very disturbing story and students feel very strong affinities with various characters, largely depending on the students' own experiences. This focuses the students on the characters and leads often to heated discussions.

2. This causes the students to reflect on the events in the story and then to extrapolate these events to their own cultures, families, communities, and so forth. Hopefully, this encourages students to question given negatives in their own societies, just as they question the given negatives in the story's society.

# "MARLENE'S ADVENTURES"

In this lovely tale, "adventure" is redefined, as that which seems novel and exciting takes second place to that which is mundane and usual—and important. While the Native reservation setting has relevance to the story, the story is universal in its recognition of the important things in life and is readable for all students.

**Vocabulary. Words crucial to understanding the story are presented in *Pre-reading Vocabulary—Context.*** However, all potentially troublesome words are listed here in the order they appear in the text, so that (1) you can easily identify words you may wish to stress and (2) you can locate them easily in the text.

# Vocabulary – "MARLENE'S ADVENTURES"

1. reins
2. horse
3. barn
4. frenzy
5. niece
6. grimace
7. feat
8. ridiculous
9. grumbling
10. surprise
11. snickering
12. liar
13. sighed
14. normal
15. predictable
16. staple
17. stationery
18. vaulted
19. straddling
20. corral
21. hoist
22. aptly
23. stirrup
24. fumble
25. foray
26. mounting
27. saddle horn
28. heave
29. cinched
30. dangling
31. gravity
32. massive
33. amble
34. semi
35. bunched
36. nimbly
37. clucked
38. pranced
39. flicked
40. giddyup
41. budge
42. plod
43. previous
44. flail
45. bucked
46. rescue
47. mustang
48. abused
49. mare
50. reservation
51. hangover
52. rosehips
53. meadow
54. tribe
55. grumble
56. bolster
57. yank
58. shrug
59. jerk
60. trot
61. grunt
62. topography
63. ignore
64. confident
65. worldly
66. generation
67. Norwegian
68. immigrant
69. divorce
70. needy
71. capable
72. boring
73. pasture
74. contemplate
75. plod
76. hesitate
77. weird
78. frustrating
79. tame
80. offense
81. desperate
82. risqué
83. provoke
84. mortified
85. imagination
86. straighten
87. groan
88. smear
89. frothy
90. hospital
91. heart attack
92. vomit
93. ignition
94. emergency room
95. collapsed
96. ambulance
97. clutching
98. rapid
99. intestinal
100. cancer
101. benign
102. prepped
103. surgery
104. retirement
105. powwow
106. blame
107. alternated
108. calm
110. resignation

**Journal Answers**

*MLA Works Cited.*

Endrezze, Anita. "Marlene's Adventures." <u>American 24-Karat Gold</u>. 2nd ed. Ed. Yvonne Sisko. New York: Longman, 2007. 231–240.

*Main Character(s).* Marlene Sullivan, the title character, is the center of this story.

*Supporting Characters.* Events swirl around Marlene and students may consider Tina, the niece who rides with Marlene and is there for much of the story, and Sonny, the husband who finally makes Marlene's adventure, main characters. Marlene's sister Darlene, who receives the hospital call, and the relevant doctor and nurses are also supporting. Old Mary, Marlene's tame horse and Frenzy, Tina's spirited steed, are also supporting here.

*Setting.* While the horse ride adventure takes place on a reservation, the setting could be placed anywhere there are riding paths and that is a drive away from the hospital. Time is relevant here as modern times are needed for the medical facilities that diagnose the benign growth and provide the surgery.

*Sequence. Here is an informal outline, but answers will vary.*

I. Marlene's horse ride adventure.
   A. Marlene sets out to do different things for her fiftieth birthday.
   B. She goes horseback riding with Tina.
   C. She discusses her next adventures.
   D. She returns back to find an emergency call.

II. Marlene's hospital adventure.
   A. She goes to the hospital to find Sonny needs surgery for cancer.
   B. It is not cancer.
   C. She realizes Sonny and her life with her family are her adventures.

*Plot. With a two-sentence limit, answers will vary.*
A woman trying new things out finds that her real adventure is in her everyday life.

*Conflicts.* Human v. nature applies in two ways. First, Marlene is aging—turning fifty—and is, therefore, seeking new things. Second, Sonny's possible cancer is given by nature. Related to that, human v. technology applies in the tension waiting for the surgery, a technological advance. Human v. herself applies here as Marlene thinks she needs new adventures to compensate for her mundane life, and then comes to realize she has had adventure all along.

*Significant Quotations.*

    a. The student should explain that "ridiculous fear" refers to Marlene's past incident with a horse when she was young. The student should note that, at fifty, Marlene is set on overcoming this fear and riding again.

    b. The student should explain that Marlene, at fifty, feels she needs new adventures. Sonny, her husband, is speaking and is telling Marlene not just to talk about new adventures but to list them and do them.

    c. The student should explain that Marlene is going to ride Old Mary, the very docile, dependable, and aged horse that Marlene compares herself to here.

    d. The student should explain that this is the moment of crisis when Marlene's adventure changes to concerns about Sonny, who has been suddenly rushed to the hospital.

    e. The student should summarize that Sonny has been through surgery, that the cancer is not cancer, and that he will heal. The student should also explain that Marlene now realizes that her everyday life is her adventure. The student may note that "stapled" together is an ironic play-on-words; Sonny owns a stationery store and sells the basics or "staples" of business correspondence that, of course, include "staples."

**Follow-up Questions. 10 Short Questions**
*These are intended for objective assessment and focus on comprehension only, purposely avoiding literary controversy.*

    1. c   It clearly states that Marlene is fifty and that, for this landmark birthday, she feels that she needs to find some adventures.

    2. b   The adventures are about trying new things that she feels she has not done and needs to do. No, she has not done everything (an extreme answer) and, no, she does not want a new life. It is her basic life that she will find is her true adventure.

    3. c   Although it is the first thing she is attempting, horseback riding is clearly stated as third on her list. First is making love in a new place and second is asking a man to dance, both of which she has clearly not done yet.

    4. b   This is important because so much of the story is about the horseback ride. Marlene has ridden as a child but has not ridden since she was a child and feels she should overcome her fear of riding.

    5. b   The incident is discussed in the story. Marlene has not been on a horse since childhood.

6. a   Mounting is not only difficult but even not successful at first, when the saddle slips off and Marlene ends up on the ground. Further, "c" is an extreme answer and "a" and "c" basically cancel each other out, in terms of test-taking strategies.

7. a   Old Mary is most certainly described as old and tame. Niece Tina's horse is the spirited one.

8. c   After all the build-up to actually getting back on a horse, Marlene finds this adventure very tame.

9. c   This is the turning point in the story. Marlene's adventure now becomes Sonny's run to the hospital. Old Mary is fine and Tina is right there with Marlene.

10. b   The student needs to infer that the real adventure, contrasted with the sought-after adventure, has been in front of Marlene all along. The horse ride is dull and, while her niece rides with her and her sister takes the emergency call, Marlene's real adventure is life with her own family.

## Follow-up Questions. 5 Significant Quotations

*These are highly focused and are intended for short answer subjective assessment of comprehension only, purposely avoiding literary controversy.*

1. The student should explain that Marlene is turning fifty and that she says she feels she should shake up her mundane life and try new things. Here, husband Sonny tells her to make of list of adventures and pursue them.

2. The student should explain that the first adventure Marlene tackles is riding a horse, something she has not done since she had an incident with a horse as a child. The student should note that Marlene rides Old Mary and that the adventure is quiet.

3. The student should explain that this is the moment when Marlene has returned from her not-so-adventurous horse ride, and that this is Marlene's sister telling Marlene that her husband has been rushed to the hospital, which now sets the tension in the story.

4. The student should explain that the word "cancer" now changes the perspective, and adventure is no longer a simple horseback ride but rather the challenge of lethal disease.

5. The student should summarize that Sonny's growth is benign and that Marlene has recognized that her real adventure is in her real, everyday life with her husband and family.

**Follow-up Questions. 2 Comprehension Essay Questions**

*These are highly focused and are intended for subjective assessment of comprehension only, purposely avoiding literary controversy or ancillary opinions. Intended to draw upon all facets of the story, 1 and 2 may repeat and/or complement each other.*

1. This focuses the student on the events in the story and the general and contrasting perception about what makes something an adventure.

2. This focuses the student on Marlene's and Sonny's characteristics. Marlene describes both as staid, a play on "stationary" (versus "stationery") and a play on "staples" as basic, mundane necessities (versus a device). The student should discuss Sonny's description of his colorful parents, Sonny's occupation, and Sonny's and Marlene's combined stability versus the excitement and newness implied in the word "adventure." It is basic life that ultimately becomes the adventure. Further, it is surgical staples that save Sonny's life.

**Discussion Questions**

*Unlike the Follow-up Questions which are intended to measure comprehension only, thereby avoiding personal opinions and/or literary controversy, these questions are intended to elicit opinions and/or debate. Answers here are only suggestions as the literary discussion may take many forms.*

1. Answers will certainly vary here. The author's intent is that the real adventure is everyday life that is often taken for granted. The students may miss the point and/or find new experiences more exciting, depending on age and class matrix.

2. After reflecting on real life as the real adventure, students may then have many views about both Marlene's insights and their own.

# "GOOD COUNTRY PEOPLE"

This story—that contrasts good with evil, sincere with insincere, intelligent with ignorant, learned with non-learned, and saccharine with sour—may best be reserved for the intermediate to advanced reader. Students are fascinated by the sinister twist in this story, but O'Connor's interweaving themes make this more complex reading.

**Vocabulary. Words crucial to understanding the story are presented in** *Pre-reading Vocabulary—Context.* However, all potentially troublesome words are listed here in the order they appear in the text, so that (1) you can easily identify words you may wish to stress and (2) you can locate them easily in the text.

# Vocabulary – "GOOD COUNTRY PEOPLE"

1. swerved
2. retract
3. imperceptible
4. receding
5. gaze
6. artificial
7. lumber
8. indistinguishable
9. ashamed
10. reference
11. applicants
12. constructive
13. perfect
14. insistence
15. hulking
16. constant
17. outrage
18. obliterated
19. stare
20. dialogue
21. patience
22. tenant
23. divorced
24. glum
25. rigid
26. shouldered
27. excused
28. attitude
29. stout
30. blank
31. hull
32. tolerate
33. resentments
34. rude
35. sullen
36. obscure
37. leer
38. blatant
39. spectacled
40. scowl
41. privacy
42. intruded
43. genius
44. Vulcan
45. triumphs
46. relish
47. beady
48. penetrated
49. fascinate
50. infections
51. assaults
52. lingering
53. stumped
54. kimono
55. indirect
56. Ph.D.
57. university
58. embossed
59. brilliant
60. bloated
61. Malebranche
62. philosophy
63. random
64. assert
65. soberness
66. phantasm
67. incantation
68. gibberish
69. ramble
70. muttered
71. Bible
72. gaunt
73. brace
74. collapse
75. prominent
76. puzzled
77. sparkling
78. burst
79. satchel
80. parlor
81. elegant
82. intimate
83. cocked
84. atheist
85. attic
86. murmured
87. honesty
88. genuine
89. groan
90. devote
91. deliberate
92. hospitality
93. courtesy
94. missionary
95. earnest
96. appraising
97. attract
98. stifle
99. wrung
100. valise
101. confronted
102. trembled
103. gesture
104. amazement
105. sty
106. chiropractor
107. inclination
108. perceive
109. sincere
110. shift
111. insinuation

112. secret
113. stumped
114. profound
115. implications
116. lain
117. insane
118. curiosity
119. fascination
120. association
121. triumphantly
122. subsiding
123. admiration
124. glittering
125. seduced
126. reckon
127. remorse
128. inferior
129. furious
130. embankment
131. acidly
132. pasture
133. glared
134. abashed
135. astonished
136. adrenaline
137. ironic
138. amusement
139. economy
140. reverently
141. contemptuous
142. awkwardly
143. loft
144. sheath
145. bale
146. methodically
147. fretting
148. ridge

149. seldom
150. committed
151. illusions
152. frowning
153. damned
154. salvation
155. whined
156. obscenity
157. shame
158. surgeon
159. sensitive
160. soul
161. innocence
162. instinct
163. wisdom
164. hoarse
165. surrendering
166. miraculously
167. jointure
168. dependent
169. function
170. shrine
171. goddess
172. mesmerized
173. coaxingly
174. lunge
175. lofty
176. indignant
177. forlornly
178. churning

# Journal Answers

*MLA Works Cited.*

O'Connor, Flannery. "Good Country People." <u>American 24-Karat Gold</u>. 2nd ed. Ed. Yvonne Sisko. New York: Longman, 2007. 249–266.

*Main Character(s).* Joy, Mrs. Hopewell's daughter with the artificial leg who renames herself Hulga, and Manley Pointer, the younger Bible salesman who carries obscene cards and a flask and steals Hulga's glasses and leg, are central to this sinister story.

*Supporting Characters.* Mrs. Hopewell, Hulga's mother who seems to live by slogans, and Mrs. Freeman, the tenant farmer's wife who loves to pry, offer continual commentary. Mrs. Freeman's daughters, Glynese and Carramae and whom Hulga calls "Glycerin and Caramel," are so "sweet" that one is pregnant by fifteen and the other is looking; they serve as foils to the sour Hulga.

*Setting.* The setting is on a southern tenant farm where both the more affluent home, the area to roam, and the barn are relevant. The setting could be a family farm anywhere.

*Sequence. Here is an informal outline, but answers will vary.*

I.  Meeting the people at breakfast.
    A.  Nosy Mrs. Freeman with the snide expression is the tenant's wife.
    B.  Mrs. Hopewell with her many slogans is the owner.
    C.  Joy is Mrs. Hopewell's daughter who has little joy and who has an artificial leg.
    D.  Glynese and Caramae are Mrs. Freeman's saccharine daughters, one becoming pregnant at fifteen and the other looking for a man.

II.  Joy renames herself Hulga.
    A.  She sees herself like Vulcan, ugly but able to control the beautiful.
    B.  She feels invaded when Mrs. Freeman calls her "Hulga."
    C.  She lost her leg in a hunting accident and holds her Ph.D. in philosophy.

III.  Manley Pointer arrives at dinnertime.
    A.  He is selling Bibles and claims to be "simple" and a "country boy."
    B.  He says he has a heart condition, like Hulga's.
    C.  Mrs. Hopewell invites him to dinner.
    D.  He walks with Hulga to the gate.

IV.  Breakfast the next day.
    A.  Mothers chatter and Mrs. Freeman refers to Hulga and Manley at the gate.

B. At the gate, Manley has seemed fascinated by Hulga and has arranged to meet her at the gate at ten after breakfast, while Hulga feels she will seduce the simple Manley.

V. Hulga and Manley meet.
   A. Manley's valise seems light.
   B. They walk across the fields to the hayloft in the barn Hulga envisioned.
   C. Manley slips her glasses in his pocket.
   D. Manley talks Hulga into showing him her leg because it makes her "brave."
   E. Manley takes off her leg and puts it in his Bible case, which only has one Bible and one hollowed Bible with obscene cards, a liquor flask, and a condom in it.
   F. Manley puts the leg in his case and leaves her, telling her she " 'ain't so smart.' "

*Plot. With a three-sentence limit, answers will vary.*
An educated young woman with an artificial leg thinks she is going to seduce a young man when, in fact, he manipulates her and takes her independence.

*Conflicts.* Certainly human v. human is involved here in the conflict between Hulga and Manley and between Hulga and Mrs. Freeman. However, human v. herself encompasses all as Hulga first chooses to be ugly and then hopes to be attractive and trusts her book knowledge which is no match for her emotional responses and Manley's manipulation.

*Significant Quotations.*

   a. The student should describe the well-intended Mrs. Hopewell and her daughter Hulga's "attitude" of negativity and ugliness. The student should explain the artificial leg that Hulga has as a result of a hunting accident when she was ten years old and that will play such a dramatic role in Hulga's downfall.

   b. The student should explain that this is Mrs. Hopewell being manipulated by Manley Pointer. When he says he is "simple" and a "country boy," Mrs. Hopewell, living by her standard that "good country people" are "salt of the earth," warms to Manley and invites him to dinner where he meets Hulga, unaware that Manley is anything but as holy as he appears.

   c. The student should explain that Hulga not only imagines herself in control of the meeting with Manley, but that she even imagines that she will have to comfort this simple boy once she has the best of him. The student should comment on the bitter irony here that he will, in fact, have the best of her.

d. This is the crucial point at which Manley manipulates Hulga into showing him how to disjoin her leg. The student should explain that Hulga is flattered by him telling her that her leg makes her "brave" and "different," thus leaving her vulnerable.

e. The student should explain that Manley now has Hulga's leg in his nearly empty Bible valise and that he is going to take off with her leg. The student should explain that when Manley opens the valise, a Bible had been hollowed and contains a whiskey flask, a deck of obscene cards, and what one would assume is a condom, all underlining the fact that Manley is not at all the holy and face-value one he pretends to be.

*Foreshadowing. Although this book is intended for the basic narrative reader and purposefully reserves deeper literary study for advanced literature classes, this question is posed to get the student thinking.* Certainly, O'Connor's names hint of roles as does the subtle allusion to Vulcan consorting with the beautiful. Contrast themes of ugly v. attractive, sincere v. insincere, learned v. non-learned also supply hints to the end result. More obvious clues are Hulga's assumption of superiority, Pointer's manipulation of both Mrs. Hopewell and Hulga, and Manley's stealth theft of Hulga's glasses and/or sight. The hollowed Bible with the flask, etc. broadly indicate the tables are turning.

## Follow-up Questions. 10 Short Questions
*These are intended for objective assessment and focus on comprehension only, purposely avoiding literary controversy.*

1. b   Glynese and Caramae, whom Hulga refers to as "Glycerin and Caramel" and who seem totally enmeshed in their men, serve as foils to Hulga's negativity and unattractiveness. She certainly knows and dislikes them.

2. b   We are clearly told that Mrs. Hopewell has hired the Freemans as tenants and that a prior reference noted Mrs. Freeman's nosiness. Mrs. Freeman is a tenant and nosy neighbor and is tacitly separated by social class. She is neither relative nor close friend.

3. a   Part of her sloganism, Mrs. Hopewell uses this term to simplistically posit what she thinks are good, salt-of-the-earth people.

4. c   Joy changes her own name, legally and without her mother's support, to Hulga.

5. b  Hulga seems to think her name is her property, her secret. She resents the prying Mrs. Freeman using it.

6. c  Hulga's dislike for Mrs. Freeman is both stated and implied. She is sarcastic toward the daughters and is sarcastic and/or out-and-out ignoring of Mrs. Freeman.

7. a  We are clearly told Hulga holds a Ph.D. in philosophy.

8. c  Although there is some talk of gadgets, Manley is selling Bibles, a crucial point in that this task makes this sinister character appear holy or, at least, reverential.

9. a  Crucial to understanding, Hulga imagines herself as seducer and consoler and master of the tryst when, in fact, Manley is the manipulative master.

10. a  Again crucial to understanding and reinforcing 9, Manley is the ultimate, manipulative master who takes Hulga's glasses and leg and independence.

## Follow-up Questions. 5 Significant Quotations

*These are highly focused and are intended for short answer subjective assessment of comprehension only, purposely avoiding literary controversy.*

1. The student should describe both the positive Mrs. Hopewell who names her daughter "Joy" and the joyless and negative daughter who renames herself "Hulga." The student should discuss that the "broad blank hull of a battleship" allusion aptly describes the stout, unattractive, and lamed Hulga.

2. The student should identify this as Manley Pointer, who manipulatively postures as a simple and saintly young man selling Bibles.

3. The student should discuss the contrast here. Hulga, with her superior education and book learning, assumes that her intelligence will carry her and that she is to be the master of the tryst when, in fact, her book learning serves her emotions and Manley Pointer's manipulations poorly.

4. The student should discuss that this is the moment Manley starts to play his hand as he sets out to steal Hulga's leg.

5. The student should explain that Manley has now stolen Hulga's glasses and her leg, which he has placed in his Bible valise. The student should discuss that the valise contains a hollowed Bible filled with a whiskey flask and obscene cards and that Manley is not who he appears. His interest has all been an insincere manipulation to gain the leg and the student should discuss that Manley now deserts Hulga, taking her leg and her dignity.

**Follow-up Questions. 2 Essay Questions**

*These are highly focused and are intended for subjective assessment of comprehension only, purposely avoiding literary controversy or ancillary opinions. Intended to draw upon all facets of the story, 1 and 2 may repeat and/or complement each other.*

1. The student should discuss Hulga's assumption that she is attractive to and smarter than Pointer, who appears simple and virtuous. She assumes she will seduce him when, if fact, he is neither as simple nor as virtuous as he seems. In the end, he controls their tryst and takes her dignity (her glasses and her leg) with him.

2. Mrs. Hopewell uses the phrase as a positive descriptive for working people. She, and the reader, assume Pointer is a hard-working and virtuous young man toiling at selling Bibles when, in fact, he is all pretense. His bag contains a bottle of liquor, playing cards, and a condom and he sets out to deflate her daughter, Hulga. The student should discuss these disparities.

**Discussion Questions**

*Unlike the Follow-up Questions which are intended to measure comprehension only, thereby avoiding personal opinions and/or literary controversy, these questions are intended to elicit opinions and/or debate. Answers here are only suggestions as the literary discussion may take many forms.*

1. This focuses students on the characters themselves. Since both characters have such exaggerated flaws, it is interesting to air students' reactions. There is often much animated discussion concerning these two very interesting and flawed characters.

2. This focuses students on the characters' behaviors and the events in the story. Defining evil and identifying that which constitutes evil in this story lead to very interesting discussions.

# CHAPTER FOUR

## *IRONY*

## "THE STORY OF AN HOUR"

Chopin's concise language and sense of the ironic combine masterfully in this tale whose brevity belies its sardonic insight. This story is accessible to almost all reading levels and makes for very lively discussion. Young men, especially, have trouble inferring that Mrs. Mallard dies of disappointment and not joy at reunion; they simply don't get it, and often need some explanation. Certainly a character study in an individual's emotions, this is placed in *Irony* because of Chopin's biting and signature irony displayed here.

**Vocabulary. Words crucial to understanding the story are presented in *Prereading Vocabulary—Context.*** However, all potentially troublesome words are listed here in the order they appear in the text so that (1) you can easily identify words you may wish to stress and (2) you can locate them easily in the text.

# Vocabulary – "THE STORY OF AN HOUR"

1. afflict
2. veil (vb.)
3. hint
4. conceal
5. intelligence
6. disaster
7. assure
8. telegram
9. hasten
10. forestall
11. paralyze
12. abandonment
13. grief
14. exhaustion
15. haunt
16. aquiver
17. peddler
18. ware
19. faintly
20. twitter
21. eave
22. sob
23. calm
24. repression
25. gaze
26. yonder
27. glance
28. reflection
29. suspension
30. subtle
31. elusive
32. tumultuous
33. approach
34. slender
35. escape
36. slightly
37. vacant
38. terror
39. keen
40. pulse
41. course (vb.)
42. monstrous
43. exalted
44. perception
45. enable
46. trivial
47. bitter
48. procession
49. absolutely
50. welcome
51. will (n.)
52. persistence
53. impose
54. cruel
55. assertion
56. recognize
57. impulse
58. implore
59. admission
60. elixir
61. fancy (n.)
62. riot
63. shudder
64. arose
65. importunity
66. triumph
67. wittingly
68. victory
69. descend
70. composed
71. amaze
72. piercing

**Journal Answers**

*MLA Works Cited.*

Chopin, Kate. "The Story of an Hour." American 24-Karat Gold. 2nd ed. Ed.
    Yvonne Sisko. New York: Longman, 2007. 277–279.

*Main Character(s).* This is a study of one woman's emotions. Louise Mallard is
the central character here.

*Supporting Characters.* Richards, Brently Mallard's friend, and Josephine,
Louise Mallard's sister, break the news to Louise and remain with her during her
reactions. Brently Mallard, Louise's husband, initiates all Louise's reactions
through his reported death and then reappearance.

*Setting.* Set in the comfortable home of a comfortable woman, the place could
be any affluent home. However, time is relevant here. The news is transferred by
word and then by appearance; this predates telephones which would have cleared
the information delay. Time is also relevant in that this is from a time when even
childless but well-off women stayed home.

*Sequence. Here is an informal outline, but answers will vary.*

  I. The train wreck.
    A. Richards hears Brently is dead in the train wreck.
    B. Richards and Josephine arrive to tell Louise Brently is dead.

  II. Louise's reaction to the wreck.
    A. Louise openly cries and then goes to her room
    B. Louise recognizes her feeling of freedom.

  III. Brently returns.
    A. Richards and Josephine are both shocked and happy for Louise.
    B. Louise dies from the shock of lost independence.
    C. Everyone assumes Louise dies from the shock of seeing her "beloved."

*Plot. With a two-sentence limit, answers will vary.*
A woman hears her husband is dead and feels freed from the marriage, only to
die from the shock of disappointment when her husband reappears.

*Conflicts.* Louise's feelings of marital entrapment are certainly human v. human and
also human v. society and/or societal assumptions. These same feeling may also be
human v. herself in that, on the one hand she stays in this marriage denying her freedom and, on the other hand, she is destroyed by her own disappointment.

*Significant Quotations.*

  a. The student should note both Louise's weak heart, which will eventually kill her, and the fact of the train wreck. The student should explain that Brently's friend, Richards, and Louise's sister, Josephine, have come to tell the news that Richards heard at the train station.

b. The student should explain that Louise at first openly cries in front of Richards and Josephine, leading all to believe that she is grief-stricken when, in fact, she now retires to be alone and discover her feelings of freedom.

c. The student should relate the spring images here to rebirth; the coming of Louise's freedom is to follow, like a rebirth for her.

d. The student should explain that Louise now turns the tables on the reader's assumptions, as she comes to feel relief at the end of her marriage.

e. The student should identify this as Brently returning home. The student should explain that Louise dies of shock not out of love returned, but rather out of freedom lost.

*Irony.* The irony in the story is that Louise is not overjoyed at Brently's return, as all assume, but rather is so devastated by her husband's return that she dies out of loss of freedom.

## Follow-up Questions. 10 Short Questions

*These are intended for objective assessment and focus on comprehension only, purposely avoiding literary controversy.*

1. c    It is Richards who is at the train station and who first hears the news.

2. b    Continuing 1, Richards hears the news at the newspaper office. This is crucial because the news is so immediate and does not wait for print publication, and phone communications are not yet available.

3. c    They are there to tell Louise the news of Brently's death.

4. a    "Overjoyed" is the wrong choice because it is her very open crying that leads us to think she is so sad about her husband's death. "Overwhelmed" is the correct descriptive here.

5. a    Central to understanding, Louise goes to her room. It is here when she is alone that the reader learns of her feelings of relief and freedom.

6. c    There is no "crying" in her room. It is the slow whispering of "'free'" that occurs.

7. b    She clearly states that she has not always loved this man, and the student should be able to infer that she has not always loved him by her feelings of relief. Further, this is good test technique training in avoiding answers that state "always."

8. c   We are clearly told he was "far from the scene" of the accident.

9. a   Crucial to understanding, it is Brently's homecoming that kills Louise.

10. c   Again crucial to understanding, Louise dies of disappointment and is, therefore, "destroyed" by Brently's return.

## Follow-up Questions. 5 Significant Quotations

*These are highly focused and are intended for short answer subjective assessment of comprehension only, purposely avoiding literary controversy.*

1. The student should explain Louise's weak heart, which will eventually kill her, and the facts about the train wreck. The student should identify Richards and Josephine as the people who bring the news of Brently's death in the train wreck.

2. The student should explain that Louise's overt tears seem to indicate—and trick the reader into believing in—Louise's grief.

3. The student should explain that Louise retires to her room alone, where she slowly starts to recognize her feelings of relief and freedom at her husband's death. What she is waiting for "fearfully" is her open admission of feeling free.

4. The student should explain that, before, Louise felt trapped in her marriage and saw it as an endless and empty future. Now with Brently's death, she sees life as an open and bright future.

5. The student should explain the dichotomy here between Louise's real feelings of relief and freedom, and society's assumed feeling of shock and love at her husband's return.

## Follow-up Questions. 2 Comprehension Essay Questions

*These are highly focused and are intended for subjective assessment of comprehension only, purposely avoiding literary controversy or ancillary opinions. Intended to draw upon all facets of the story, 1 and 2 may repeat and/or complement each other.*

1. Summarizing all that happens within a short hour, the student should relate the events in logical sequence from the misinformation about the crash, through the feelings of freedom, to Mrs. Mallard's untimely death.

2. Again, the student will need to summarize the events of the story in logical order to explain the phrase. The student will then need to discuss the irony of the marital misconceptions that Chopin presents.

## Discussion Questions

*Unlike the Follow-up Questions which are intended to measure comprehension only, thereby avoiding personal opinions and/or literary controversy, these questions are intended to elicit opinions and/or debate. Answers here are only suggestions as the literary discussion may take many forms.*

1. This makes for very interesting discussion. Students, as we all do, often tend to take societal dictates and assumptions for granted. Knowing that one can even look at these assumptions is often a real leap for students. Reviewing the assumptions in this story focuses students on the events in the story. Reviewing assumptions in their own society takes the students far beyond the story.

2. This is always a very interesting discussion, because some students simply do not get why she dies. Some tend to find it hard to accept that Mrs. Mallard does not love her husband and their sympathies lie with Mr. Mallard. Others find it all too easy to accept that she does not love him, and their sympathies lie with Mrs. Mallard.

## "GIFTS OF THE MAGI"

This wonderful tale is a must for all readers. You may find some students have already read this in adapted form (with watered down vocabulary and condensed language), but here it is in O. Henry's lively and civilized tongue. This, of course, draws much active discussion and interesting writing and all—those who *think* they have read it and those who are reading it for the first time—enjoy this classic tale.

**Vocabulary. Words crucial to understanding the story are presented in *Prereading Vocabulary—Context*.** However, all potentially troublesome words are listed here in the order they appear in the text so that (1) you can easily identify words you may wish to stress and (2) you can locate them easily in the text.

# Vocabulary – "GIFTS OF THE MAGI"

1. Magi
2. grocer
3. butcher
4. cheek
5. imputation
6. parsimony
7. imply
8. flop
9. shabby
10. howl
11. instigate
12. moral
13. reflection
14. gradually
15. flat (n.)
16. beggar (vb.)
17. mendicancy
18. mortal
19. coax
20. appertain
21. fling
22. former
23. prosperity
24. shrunk
25. modest
26. attend
27. dully
28. calculate
29. sterling
30. worthy
31. honor
32. agile
33. observe
34. rapid
35. sequence
36. longitude
37. accurate

38. conception
39. slender
40. whirl
41. brilliant
42. possession
43. Queen of Sheba
44. King Solomon
45. janitor
46. pluck
47. cascade
48. garment
49. falter
50. flutter
51. chilly
52. rosy
53. hash
54. metaphor
55. ransack
56. platinum
57. fob
58. chaste
59. meretricious
60. anxious
61. sly
62. intoxication
63. prudence
64. ravages
65. generosity
66. tremendous
67. mammoth
68. task
69. truant
70. critical
71. chorus
72. burden
73. quail
74. terrify

75. horror
76. sentiment
77. stare
78. peculiar
79. wriggle
80. patent
81. labor
82. curious
83. idiocy
84. discreet
85. scrutiny
86. inconsequential
87. wit
88. assertion
89. nimble
90. ecstatic
91. hysterical
92. wail
93. lord
94. worship
95. tortoise
96. vanish
97. tress
98. covet
99. singe
100. ardent
101. dandy
102. obey
103. privilege
104. exchange
105. doubt
106. duplication
107. chronicle
108. sacrifice
109. wise

**Journal Answers**

*MLA Works Cited.*

Henry, O. "Gifts of the Magi." <u>American 24-Karat Gold</u>. 2nd ed. Ed. Yvonne
      Sisko. New York: Longman, 2007. 288–292.

*Main Character(s).* Della and Jim Young—Mr. and Mrs. James Dillingham
Young—are the poor people who must sell their prized possessions for each
other, and are the central characters here.

*Supporting Characters.* Mme. Sofronie who buys Della's hair is the only stated
supporting character, although the broker who buys Jim's watch and those who
sell the fob chain and the combs can be inferred.

*Setting.* The setting is a rather shabby apartment in a large city. Both shabby, for
the poverty, and large city, for the anonymity, are relevant.

*Sequence. Here is an informal outline, but answers will vary.*

   I. Della buys Jim's gift.
     A. Della sells her hair.
     B. Della uses the money to buy Jim a fob chain for his pocket watch.
  II. Jim buys Della's gift.
     A. Jim sells his pocket watch.
     B. Jim uses the money to buy Della combs for her now cut hair.
 III. Both end up happy without their prized possessions.

*Plot. With a three-sentence limit, answers will vary.*
A young wife sells her hair to buy her husband a chain for his watch, while he
sells his watch to buy combs for her hair.

*Conflicts.* Human v. society may be relevant for their poverty, but one wants to
say human v. things because the possessions, given in generosity, are at the heart
of this gentle but ironic conflict here.

*Significant Quotations.*

   a. The student should explain the Young's poverty which sets them both in the
      position of not having enough money with which to buy Christmas gifts.
   b. The student should explain that this describes the Young's most prized pos-
      sessions—her hair and his watch.
   c. The student should explain that Della sells her hair to buy Jim a fob chain
      for his watch.
   d. The student should explain that Jim has sold his watch to buy the combs she

so liked for her now gone hair.

   e. The student should explain that O. Henry leaves us on a positive note and with the message that things aren't everything.

*Irony.* The irony is that Della sells her hair to buy a chain for the watch Jim no longer owns, while Jim sells the watch to buy combs for the hair Della no longer has.

## Follow-up Questions. 10 Short Questions
*These are intended for objective assessment and focus on comprehension only, purposely avoiding literary controversy.*

   1. c  The references to Coney Island and Broadway suggest New York. Further, this is also a test if the student read the biography which clearly links O. Henry's stories to New York.

   2. b  Indicating understanding, it is poverty that necessitates the sales.

   3. b  Indicating understanding, Della's hair is her prized possession.

   4. c  Indicating understanding, Jim's watch is his prized possession.

   5. a  Indicating understanding, Della wants to sell her hair so that she can purchase the fob for Jim's watch. She has admired but she does not intend to buy the combs.

   6. c  Continuing 5 and measuring close reading, Della wants to buy the fob for Jim. It is Jim—not Della—who wants to buy the combs and Jim already owns the watch.

   7. b  Jim wants to pawn the watch. The other answers are Della's actions.

   8. a  Continuing 7 and retesting close reading, Jim has pawned the watch and Della is buying the fob. It is Jim who buys the combs.

   9. c  We are clearly told that the gifts are for Christmas.

  10. b  The reader can infer that the Youngs enjoy Christmas, despite the irony of the gifts.

## Follow-up Questions. 5 Significant Quotations
*These are highly focused and are intended for short answer subjective assessment of comprehension only, purposely avoiding literary controversy.*

   1. The student should explain that the Youngs are quite poor and do not have money to spare, which causes the selling of the precious hair and watch.

2. The student should explain the two possessions: Della's hair and Jim's watch.

3. The student should explain that this is the moment when Della is selling her hair so that she can buy the chain for Jim's watch.

4. The student should explain that Jim has sold his watch in order to buy Della the combs she no longer needs for the missing hair.

5. The student should explain that, in spite of the lost possessions, O. Henry leaves us positively and feeling things are not everything.

## Follow-up Questions. 2 Comprehension Essay Questions

*These are highly focused and are intended for subjective assessment of comprehension only, purposely avoiding literary controversy or ancillary opinions. Intended to draw upon all facets of the story, 1 and 2 may repeat and/or complement each other.*

1. Focusing on the events, the student should discuss the events in logical sequence and explain the ironies of the gifts.

2. Focusing on the objects, the student should explain the gifts and the ironies therein. The student should relate this to the title noting the well if not wisely given gifts.

## Discussion Questions

*Unlike the Follow-up Questions which are intended to measure comprehension only, thereby avoiding personal opinions and/or literary controversy, these questions are intended to elicit opinions and/or debate. Answers here are only suggestions as the literary discussion may take many forms.*

1. This focuses students on the characters and makes them look at the characters more closely. Discussions on this topic range in many areas as students reflect not only on the characters but on themselves as well.

2. This focuses students on the events in the story and the very ironies themselves. This also raises general communication issues and students tend to take rather strong stands based on their own experiences.

## "THE RANSOM OF RED CHIEF"

In one of America's truly funny stories that has inspired later cinema variations, a kidnapping goes bad when the boy kidnapped is such a nightmare that the kidnappers end up paying the father in order to return the boy. It may be prudent to note that this was written in a simpler time when kidnapping was not the threat and did not inspire the fear that it does today. Further, the boy adopts a nickname based on a Native American stereotype to demonstrate his dominance and the student may not be familiar with the game of Cowboys and Indians. Given these considerations, "Red Chief" is humorous in both actions and ironic false assumptions. The interest and the humor make this generally accessible to all students.

**Vocabulary. Words crucial to understanding the story are presented in *Prereading Vocabulary—Context.*** However, all potentially troublesome words are listed here in the order they appear in the text, so that (1) you can easily identify words you may wish to stress and (2) you can locate them easily in the text.

# Vocabulary – "THE RANSOM OF RED CHIEF"

1. kidnapping
2. apparition
3. flannel
4. summit
5. inhabitants
6. deleterious
7. Maypole
8. capital
9. fraudulent
10. scheme
11. philoprogenitiveness
12. radius
13. constable
14. lackadaisical
15. diatribe
16. victim
17. prominent
18. mortgage
19. stern
20. foreclose
21. bas-relief
22. freckles
23. ransom
24. cedar
25. cave
26. provisions
27. buggy
28. bruise
29. buzzard
30. paleface
31. plains
32. Palestine
33. scalped
34. captive
35. Geronimo
36. christen
37. braves
38. stake
39. 'possum
40. whipped
41. pesky
42. redskin
43. scout
44. shiver
45. quilts
46. crackle
47. rustle
48. stealthy
49. whoop
50. yawp
51. vocal
52. humiliating
53. emit
54. desperate
55. incontinently
56. liar
57. imp
58. rowdy
59. dote
60. reconnoitre
61. contiguous
62. vicinity
63. yeomanry
64. scythes
65. pitchfork
66. dastardly
67. ploughing
68. mule
69. courier
70. hither and yon
71. tidings
72. distracted
73. sylvan
74. somnolent
75. pervading
76. external
77. cocoanut
78. boxed
79. neighbors
80. rattled
81. sullenly
82. village
83. peremptory
84. outrage
85. amused
86. affection
87. relieve
88. acceded
89. collaborated
90. absolutely
91. solitary
92. messenger
93. treachery
94. comply
95. suspiciously
96. elder
97. surreptitiously
98. mossy
99. glade
100. renegade
101. masculine
102. proclivities
103. egotism
104. predominance
105. martyr
106. depredation
107. palatable
108. substitute

109. cauterize
110. features
111. chronic
112. professional
113. concluded
114. square
115. lantern
116. proposition
117. inclined
118. impudent
119. appealing
120. Bedlam
121. liberal
122. ewe
123. moccasins
124. abstracting
125. calliope
126. leech
127. porous
128. trippingly

## Journal Answers

*MLA Works Cited.*

Henry, O. "The Ransom of Red Chief." American 24-Karat Gold. 2nd ed. Ed. Yvonne Sisko. New York: Longman, 2007. 301–310.

*Main Character(s).* There are three main characters. Sam, who seems to be the brains in the scheme, and Bill, who is the hapless playmate of Johnny, are two down-on-their-luck fellows who decide to make some money they need for a scam by kidnapping a town leader's son. Johnny Dorset is the boy who is kidnapped and who proves to be a terror.

*Supporting Characters.* Ebenezer Dorset, Johnny's father, is the major support. He is contacted for the ransom and his response, offering to take Johnny back for a fee, initiates the central irony. The townspeople in Poplar Grove, where Sam erroneously assumes Summit is upset, are active while the town of Summit, the immediate Dorset neighbors, and the mythical sheriff and posse are all implied.

*Setting.* O. Henry tell us that this is set in Alabama, although anywhere out west with small towns and open space is applicable. Time is more relevant, as this is set in a simpler time when all the characters and the kidnapping itself are comical.

*Sequence. Here is an informal outline, but answers will vary.*

I. Kidnapping scheme.
   A. Sam and Bill plan to make money by kidnapping a "prominent" person's child.
   B. Sam and Bill easily lure Johnny Dorset.
   C. Johnny proves to be a nightmare.
      1. Throws rocks and other physical abuse.
      2. Talks incessantly.
      3. Threatens to scalp and/or burn the men at the stake.
      4. Rides Bill.

II. Ransom.
   A. Sam and Bill reduce the ransom from $2000 to $1500 to get rid of Johnny.
   B. Sam plans and executes the delivery and response.
   C. Sam listens for the response in Poplar Grove and erroneously assumes Summit is upset.

III. Response.
   A. Father counter-offers to accept $250 to take Johnny back.
   B. Bill pleads and Sam agrees.

C. Sam and Bill pay Dorset $250 to take Johnny back.

*Plot. With a two-sentence limit, answers will vary.*
Hoping to make money by kidnapping a wealthy boy, two men end up having to pay the father in order to get rid of the boy.

*Conflicts.* Human v. human certainly applies to the abuse Bill receives from Johnny. Human v. human(s) also applies to Dorset refusing to pay and accepting money only. Human v. society may be relevant as the reader assumes the ransom process and the wrongful nature of kidnapping which, in fact, turn humorous.

*Significant Quotations.*

   a. The student should describe the kidnapping plans here.
   b. The student should discuss Johnny's uproarious behavior and the beating Bill is taking as a result of trying to entertain Johnny.
   c. The student should discuss the humor in this scene. Bill has taken Johnny back, assuming Johnny will return to his house on his own. In fact, Johnny is having such a good time that he follows Bill right back to their hideout.
   d. The student should explain that this is Ebenezer Dorset's response. Not only is he not going to pay the ransom, but he wants money to accept Johnny back and even advises the kidnappers to return Johnny at night so that the neighbors do not see his return.
   e. This is the unhappy outcome for Sam and Bill. The student should explain that the kidnapping that was supposed to make them money has, in fact, cost them money.

*Irony.* The student should discuss the kidnapping that costs rather than profits the kidnappers. Part of this discussion should include Sam's misinterpretation in Poplar Grove (he assumes Summit is concerned when, in fact, it is implied that the town is relieved to have a break) and Sam's vigilance for a nonexistent sheriff and posse.

**Follow-up Questions. 10 Short Questions**
*These are intended for objective assessment and focus on comprehension only, purposely avoiding literary controversy.*

   1. c   The student should be able to infer that these are two, as they call themselves, "Desperate Men" who need money.
   2. a   There is no indication whatsoever that Johnny resists or wants to stay home. Rather, this becomes a welcome adventure for him.

3. b   Johnny is absolutely delighted with the whole adventure. In fact, when Bill tries to return Johnny home, Johnny follows Bill back to the hideout.

4. c   Bill is absolutely bruised and scraped from play. He is having no fun playing.

5. a   The reader should be able to discern that it is Sam who does all the planning and communication. Bill stays to take care of Johnny and, of course, Johnny is the "victim."

6. b   He erroneously assumes that the talk of Summit is concern. The student should be able to infer that Summit is, if not overjoyed, at least happy to have a break from Johnny. This is all part of the humor and the irony in a kidnapping gone awry.

7. a   Reinforcing 6, while Sam assumes Summit is concerned, the student should infer that, in fact, Summit is happy or, at least, relieved at a break from Johnny.

8. b   Originally they planned on $2000, but Bill pleads to reduce this to $1500 for fear Dorset will not take Johnny back. 8, 9, and 10 check accurate reading. $2000 is the original amount that is discarded on Bill's pleas; $1500 is the ransom amount; and $250 is the amount Dorset demands to be paid to take back Johnny.

9. c   There is no payment and no sheriff called. Dorset offers to take Johnny back if the kidnappers will pay him.

10. c   Instead of realizing any profit, Bill and Sam pay Dorset to take back Johnny. In fact, they do so at nighttime so that the neighbors will not see the return, at Dorset's suggestion, and they then ask Dorset to hold on to Johnny so that they can get out of town without Johnny following them.

## Follow-up Questions. 5 Significant Quotations
*These are highly focused and are intended for short answer subjective assessment of comprehension only, purposely avoiding literary controversy.*

1. The student should discuss the plan to make money by kidnapping the son of a wealthy citizen, Ebenezer Dorset.

2. The student should discuss Johnny's untoward behavior. Here specifically, Sam wakens before Johnny for fear Johnny will try to burn him at the stake. The physical abuse especially Bill receives from Johnny and Johnny's incessant talking all add up to why Sam and Bill will be desperate to return Johnny. Johnny's poor behavior is all part of the irony.

3. This is from the ransom note. The student should discuss the ransom reduction and Sam's careful plan to communicate and execute the ransom.

4. The student should discuss Sam's misunderstanding. Sam thinks Summit and the Dorsets are upset and will gladly pay for Johnny's return. In fact, the student can infer that neither the town nor the parents are too upset by Johnny's temporary absence.

5. This is Dorset's counteroffer. The student should discuss the irony here: not only will the kidnappers not profit but they will, in fact, have to pay to get Johnny accepted back home.

## Follow-up Questions. 2 Comprehension Essay Questions

*These are highly focused and are intended for subjective assessment of comprehension only, purposely avoiding literary controversy or ancillary opinions. Intended to draw upon all facets of the story, 1 and 2 may repeat and/or complement each other.*

1. Focusing on the events, the student should present the events in logical order (the plan, Johnny's willing and overzealous play, the ransom amount, and the final amount that has to be paid to return Johnny) to demonstrate the central irony of the story.

2. Focusing on analysis, the student should discuss both Sam's and Bill's errors. They assume that they will make money, that entertaining Johnny will be much easier than it is, etc. Sam's specific error is in assuming that Summit and that the Dorsets are deeply upset by Johnny's absence when, in fact, one can assume that all are, at least, relieved at his temporary absence. Bill's specific error is in assuming that Johnny will want to go home when, in fact, Johnny simply follows Bill back to the hideout.

## Discussion Questions

*Unlike the Follow-up Questions which are intended to measure comprehension only, thereby avoiding personal opinions and/or literary controversy, these questions are intended to elicit opinions and/or debate. Answers here are only suggestions as the literary discussion may take many forms.*

1. This wonderful illustration presents the basic elements of the story and focuses the students on the characters, the events, and interplay between the characters. Sam and Bill are both beside themselves in dealing with Johnny, who seems never to want to go home, and are, after all, criminals, but then

again they are likeable criminals. The story via the illustration raises questions about protagonists and antagonists as the students reflect on the events and the characters themselves.

2. The students may have already identified the obvious irony in the Essay Questions of the kidnappers having to pay to return Johnny. However, there are other ironies that discussion should help the students discover. Johnny being delighted with staying away from home, rather than wanting to return home, is one. Sam thinking Johnny's absence is of great concern when it is not is another. Yet another is Bill originally wanting more and then wanting less and then wanting to pay for the return. Bill trying to return Johnny and Johnny following him back is another. Sam planning carefully for a posse that does not exist is another. Even the town in the low valley is named, of course, "Summit." The students should be able to note the humor in these twists.

# "THE WONDERFUL OLD GENTLEMAN"

Parker writes from a gentler and slower time, but her biting irony rings true today. Although she uses more formal language and sprinkles in many vocabulary terms, the clear characters in this story and the escalating atrocities carry the students along. All respond to the inherent injustices.

**Vocabulary. Words crucial to understanding the story are presented in *Prereading Vocabulary—Context.*** However, all potentially troublesome words are listed here in the order they appear in the text, so that (1) you can easily identify words you may wish to stress and (2) you can locate them easily in the text.

# Vocabulary – "THE WONDERFUL OLD GENTLEMAN"

1. striven
2. successful
3. admirably
4. museum
5. tomb
6. predecessor
7. succumb
8. scheme
9. enthusiast
10. achieve
11. eventual
12. result
13. modify
14. weaving
15. stale
16. mustard
17. twinkling
18. smear
19. sensitive
20. battered
21. tortured
22. profile
23. clotted
24. cumbersome
25. creaking
26. wrung
27. dull
28. tapestry
29. accumulate
30. crevice
31. perpetually
32. strained
33. discreetly
34. confusion
35. scroll
36. scale
37. elephant
38. tedious
39. mantel
40. peasant
41. ingeniously
42. eternal
43. wrinkled
44. cruel
45. careen
46. ferociously
47. devoted
48. religious
49. Crucifixion
50. lavish
51. ghastly
52. sepia
53. martyrdom
54. writhing
55. bristling
56. agonized
57. wan
58. blizzard
59. contributions
60. stationer
61. relentlessly
62. automobile
63. shattered
64. opportunity
65. conversation
66. ornament
67. gilt
68. Laocoön
69. savage
70. awe
71. Oriental
72. grotesque
73. bulging
74. gape
75. oppressed
76. accustom
77. admirer
78. surrounding
79. morbid
80. aristocratic
81. graciously
82. patronize
83. tolerance
84. reference
85. expectancy
86. tumblers
87. resolutely
88. occasion
89. informal
90. augmented
91. courteous
92. competent
93. tactful
94. polite
95. conscientiously
96. pince-nez
97. handkerchief
98. compliment
99. crepe de Chine
100. lapis-lazuli
101. olivine
102. topaz
103. amethyst
104. lorgnette
105. studiously
106. attired
107. authority
108. monogram
109. condolence
110. predicted
111. rumpled

112. verdict
113. distraught
114. elaborately
115. coiffure
116. straggling
117. Persian
118. exposition
119. servant
120. gathered
121. board
122. adjoining
123. appropriate
124. favoritism
125. hyacinth
126. chauffeur
127. accompany
128. neglected
129. affection
130. disturbing
131. telegraph
132. funeral
133. ruddy
134. jovial
135. clerical
136. intervention
137. salary
138. indubitably
139. amended
140. frock
141. eagerly
142. draft
143. summarized
144. chuckling
145. reminiscently
146. temper
147. vied
148. intelligence

149. anecdote
150. precocious
151. racket
152. nuisance
153. triumphantly
154. edged
155. composedly
156. wearily
157. cracker-jack
158. hastening
159. black sheep
160. frankly
161. sulky
162. fare
163. affairs
164. splendid
165. will (n.)
166. plait
167. reception
168. formal
169. bewilderment
170. reproved
171. realize
172. humor
173. whist
174. furious
175. extinction
176. crimson
177. whimpering
178. collapsed
179. passionate

## Journal Answers

*MLA Works Cited.*

Parker, Dorothy. "The Wonderful Old Gentleman." <u>American 24-Karat Gold</u>. 2nd ed. Ed. Yvonne Sisko. New York: Longman, 2007. 319–329.

*Main Character(s).* Allie Bain, the poorer sister and devoted daughter, and Hattie Whittaker, the richer sister and superficial daughter, are the center here. Although he never actually appears, the student may consider the Old Gentleman, the nasty father, central as all the actions and the very title revolve around his behaviors.

*Supporting Characters.* If the student has not named the Old Gentleman, due to lack of actual appearance, he certainly must be named here. Mr. Lewis Bain, Allie's devoted husband, may be mentioned as a main character as he participates in all; if he is not listed as main, he is certainly supporting. The Bains' son, Paul, is supporting in that his exile underlines the Old Gentleman's nastiness and Allie's blind submission to her demanding father. Matt, the sisters' brother, supports as does Paul, in that the father's treatment and eventual ostracism of Matt underlines the father's nastiness and Hattie's superficiality that fails to recognize family bonds. Mr. Fuller, who fires Matt, and Miss Chester, the nurse who tends the Old Gentleman, are also supporting. Hattie's husband, Clint, serves to reinforce Hattie's superficiality while the doctor predicts the Old Gentleman's demise is near, which brings the sisters to Allie's living room.

*Setting.* This is set in a drab and gloomy living room in a home, on the one hand, big enough to house the Bains, the Old Gentleman, and a nurse but, on the other hand, described as shabby. Any town with a richer section, implied to Hattie, and a poorer if genteel section will do.

*Sequence. Here is an informal outline, but answers will vary.*

I. Family in the living room.
   A. Allie and Lewis Bain are seated in their antiquated and gloomy living room.
   B. Hattie Whittaker, Allie's sister, has joined them dressed in her funerary best.
   C. All are waiting for their father to die upstairs, as the doctor has predicted.

II. The Old Gentleman living with Allie and Lewis.
   A. Hattie says it doesn't look right for him to live with a nurse when he has daughters, so Hattie sends him to Allie.
   B. He brings enough to make himself comfortable.

C. He pays no board and contributes nothing.

D. He criticizes Allie and won't allow the Bains to have friends in.

E. He drives out Paul, his grandson and the Bains' son.

III. The Old Gentleman's unfairness to his children.

A. He criticizes Allie who provides his home and praises Hattie who sends postcards.

B. He sabotaged his son, Matt, and Hattie says don't call Matt for the funeral.

C. His wife worked hard, in order not to upset him.

IV. The Old Gentleman's will.

A. He leaves his wealth to Hattie, the rich and unconcerned sister.

B. He leaves his junk and forgives a two hundred dollar loan to Allie and Lewis, the poorer and devoted children.

C. Matt is out of it altogether.

V. The Old Gentleman dies.

A. Miss Chester, the nurse, announces his death.

B. Hattie, uncaring, is serene.

C. Allie is distraught and must be helped up the stairs.

*Plot. With a three-sentence limit, answers will vary.*

The poorer sister takes her aging father in and sacrifices for him, while the richer sister does nothing and, in the end, he leaves his wealth to the rich and uncaring daughter.

*Conflicts.* Human v. human applies here between the sisters as Allie's sacrifice loses to Hattie's superficiality. Human v. human applies to the Old Gentleman and all his family, it would seem, except Hattie. He makes inordinate demands on Allie and Lewis, he removes Paul from the Bains' own home, he sabotages his own son, and he seems to have had his wife servile.

*Significant Quotations.*

a. Measuring the context word "handkerchief," the student should discuss Hattie's carefully chosen funerary clothes with Allie's real life casualness. The student should contrast the poorer and devoted Allie with the rich and superficial Hattie.

b. The student should contrast Hattie's superficial devotion with Allie's real devotion. Hattie, who has a large home and means, says it doesn't look right that the father is not tended by daughters and then ships him off to Allie who has little room and less money.

c. The student should discuss the father's demands on the Bains. He will not let them have friends in and even drives their son, Paul, away, much to Allie's sorrow. Superficial Hattie, with seemingly no concept of true familial feelings, says not only was sending Paul away no problem but, in fact, his vacancy has made room for the father's nurse.

d. The student should explain the father's sabotage of his own son, Matt. When Matt had a job, the father went to his boss and told him about his son's drinking and poor behavior which, of course, cost Matt his job. The student should explain that Matt has resettled elsewhere and that Allie feels he should be called for the funeral while Hattie, of course, is perfectly happy to dismiss him away.

e. This is the bite and the student should explain that the father has left all his wealth to very undeserving Hattie. For Allie and Lewis who have put up with all his nastiness, he has left the old stuff he brought with him and he has forgiven Lewis a loan—not a gift, a loan—for two hundred dollars. Matt, of course, receives nothing.

*Irony.* The irony is that the poorer daughter, who sacrifices for the father and who cares about him, receives next to nothing while the rich daughter, who has done nothing and seems to care little, receives the wealth.

### Follow-up Questions. 10 Short Questions
*These are intended for objective assessment and focus on comprehension only, purposely avoiding literary controversy.*

1. b  Indicating understanding, between the sisters the Bains are poorer.
2. a  Indicating understanding, the well-dressed, bejeweled Hattie with her servants and chauffeur is richer.
3. c  Indicating understanding, the Old Gentleman is father to both Allie and Hattie which sets up the conflict here.
4. a  Indicating understanding, the student must understand that he lives with the long-suffering Bains.
5. c  We are clearly told Paul must leave because the Old Gentleman cannot abide his friends and noise.
6. a  Indicating understanding, this is an example of the father's outrageous demands on the Bains. The student can infer Allie is upset as she raises the subject, rues his absence, and sadly looks at his picture. The student can further infer that Allie is a caring person and the absence of her son is hard on her.

7. c   Indicating understanding, there is a rather tongue-in-cheek description of the Old Gentleman going to Matt's boss and telling him about Matt's drinking and poor behavior. While Hattie says how good the father was to buy Matt an occasional suit, the student should be able to infer that the father has been terrible to and probably driven off his son. Even if the student does not understand the word "undermines," the father certainly has not been good to his son and does not see him at all.

8. a   Matt has disappeared, probably out of disgust, and Hattie's idea of devotion is to send a car around so the father can go for a ride—not to her house, by the way. The student should infer, from all the abuse Allie takes and yet still tends to her father, that she is the only one who really cares about him.

9. b   This is the irony of the story. After all of Allie's devotion and Hattie's lack of it, it is Hattie, who needs the money least, that the father leaves the money to.

10. b   Hattie says he does not play favorites, but his favoritism for Hattie is implied by his praise for her, contrasted with his criticism of the sacrificing Allie, and his entrusting Hattie with his will and his wealth, contrasted with the pittance he leaves Allie, who has not even been allowed to see the will. His unfairness is the base of the irony.

## Follow-up Questions. 5 Significant Quotations

*These are highly focused and are intended for short answer subjective assessment of comprehension only, purposely avoiding literary controversy.*

1. The student should describe Allie, poor yet devoted to sacrificing for her father, and contrast her with the superficial Hattie whose hankie is not wet at all. The student should explain that Allie cares about her father while Hattie seems to have no familial feelings.

2. The student should explain that Hattie, with a large home and money, decides it doesn't look right that the father is not tended to by his daughters. She sends him off to Allie, with a small home and little money to make the sacrifices. This demonstrates Hattie's superficiality.

3. The student should explain that the father made many demands on the Bains and the supremely outrageous demand is this one. The father has driven his grandson out of the house and the student should explain this hurts Allie and is a supreme sacrifice on her part. Hattie's reaction is that it is no big deal and simply made room for the father's nurse.

4. The student should identify Matt as the sisters' brother and Old Gentleman's son whom the Old Gentleman drove away years ago. The student should tell the story of the Old Gentleman sabotaging Matt by telling his boss that he drinks. The student should note that Matt has moved away and that Hattie does not want to tell her own brother about his father's funeral because she feels his wife may embarrass the family.

5. The student should explain that this is the bitter irony. The father shares the will with and is leaving his wealth to Hattie, who doesn't need the money and who seems to have little feelings for him and who has sacrificed nothing, while to Allie, who does need the money and has housed him and sacrificed for him and who cares about him, he leaves next to nothing.

**Follow-up Questions. 2 Comprehension Essay Questions**
*These are highly focused and are intended for subjective assessment of comprehension only, purposely avoiding literary controversy or ancillary opinions. Intended to draw upon all facets of the story, 1 and 2 may repeat and/or complement each other.*

1. Focusing on the events, the student should relate the events of the story in logical sequence and note the biting irony the actions produce.

2. Focusing on the characters, the student should discuss the various characters and the biting irony in the will.

**Discussion Questions**
*Unlike the Follow-up Questions which are intended to measure comprehension only, thereby avoiding personal opinions and/or literary controversy, these questions are intended to elicit opinions and/or debate. Answers here are only suggestions as the literary discussion may take many forms.*

1. This asks the students to reflect on the ironies and injustices that swirl around these characters. Students generally have very strong reactions to the Old Gentleman's favoritism, Mrs. Whittaker's arrogance, and the long-suffering Bains.

2. This focuses students on the characters themselves, extending the ironies and injustices discussed in 1 and setting a clear contrast between the sisters. The well cared for Mrs. Whittaker poses a strong contrast to her overworked sister. Students should be able to paint a portrait of Mrs. Bain in contrast to her sister, based on details in the story.

## "SWEAT"

Delia emerges as Hurston's resilient female, while Sykes encapsulates the ignorant and arrogant male. Hurston's writing always contains hope and Delia triumphs over abuse and indignation and is the hope: She will survive. Further,
Hurston's wonderfully rich, local language fairly sings through this story.
Although the conversation demands close reading, students enjoy this tale that
sees wrongs righted.

**Vocabulary. Words crucial to understanding the story are presented in *Pre-
reading Vocabulary—Context.*** However, all potentially troublesome words are
listed here in the order they appear in the text, so that (1) you can easily identify words you may wish to stress and (2) you can locate them easily in the text.

# Vocabulary – "SWEAT"

1. soil
2. soak
3. hamper
4. bundle
5. squat
6. heap
7. buckboard
8. limp
9. slither
10. terror
11. whip
12. mirth
13. glare
14. galvanize
15. truculent
16. commence
17. threaten
18. breeches
19. stoop
20. sag
21. sacrament
22. snort
23. hypocrite
24. Sabbath
25. roughly
26. helter-skelter
27. dismay
28. meek
29. defy
30. strapping
31. hulk
32. vittle
33. seize
34. skillet
35. defensive
36. cow (vb.)
37. tote
38. foremost
39. awe
40. sidle
41. debris
42. matrimonial
43. image
44. brutal
45. numerous
46. limb
47. harsh
48. reap
49. sow
50. spiritual
51. triumphant
52. indifferent
53. hurl
54. dribble
55. shaggy
56. sardine
57. humble
58. wring
59. grunt
60. civic
61. virtue
62. retort
63. jackknife
64. magnificent
65. feast
66. frequent
67. assure
68. abominate
69. portly
70. Gethsemane
71. Calvary
72. villager
73. nullify
74. interlude
75. timid
76. repulse
77. breach
78. agape
79. smite
80. wither
81. stumble
82. rattlesnake
83. fang
84. obstreperous
85. superior
86. digest
87. scimitar
88. avert
89. fury
90. broach
91. deliberate
92. amazement
93. whip (vb.)
94. depart
95. quarrel
96. hitch
97. emotional
98. domestic
99. misery
100. suppression
101. inhibition
102. hamper
103. horror
104. terror
105. sluggish
106. insane
107. vigorous
108. sprawl
109. gibbering
110. coherent
111. stalk

112. introspection
113. retrospection
114. calm
115. demolish
116. descend
117. crouch
118. tremendous
119. whirr
120. ventriloquist
121. paralyze
122. primitive
123. instinct
124. chimpanzee
125. stricken
126. gorilla
127. rage
128. recognize
129. intermittent
130. reptile
131. punctuate
132. abrupt
133. crept
134. despair
135. flabby
136. moan
137. approach
138. swollen
139. surge
140. pity
141. extinguish

**Journal Answers**

*MLA Works Cited.*

Hurston, Zora Neale. "Sweat." American 24-Karat Gold. 2nd ed. Ed. Yvonne
    Sisko. New York: Longman, 2007. 338–348.

*Main Character(s).* Delia, the hardworking and loyal wife, and Sykes, the ne'er-
do-well and philandering husband, are the core of this story. The rattlesnake may
be placed here as it is certainly central to the action, although the student may
consider it supporting or a prop. It is central to the irony.

*Supporting Characters.* Bertha, Sykes's girlfriend, adds to the indignity and fuels
the anger in the marriage. The men on Joe Clark's porch serve as a chorus, punc-
tuating the good in Delia and the bad in Sykes.

*Setting.* Set in a small and rural southern town, any rural town small enough for
most to know each other will do. If the student has not discussed the rattlesnake
as a character, then it certainly must appear here as a prop.

*Sequence. Here is an informal outline, but answers will vary.*

I.  Sykes abuses Delia.
    A. He scares her with his whip.
    B. He mixes her work (laundry pile) up.
    C. She stands up to him and he does not hit her.
    D. She works and he does nothing.
    E. He has another woman.

II. The men in town talk about Delia and Sykes.
    A. They respect Delia.
    B. They think Sykes is worthless.

III. Sykes brings the snake home.
    A. Delia is afraid of the snake and wants it out.
    B. Sykes wants Delia out, but she is not leaving.
    C. The snake escapes and scares Delia out of the house.
    D. The snake bites Sykes and he calls Delia for help.
    E. Delia does not respond until too late.
    F. Sykes will die from the snakebite.

*Plot. With a three-sentence limit, answers will vary.*
An abusive husband brings home a rattlesnake to scare off his wife, but the snake
ends up destroying the husband.

*Conflicts.* Human v. human certainly applies in the constant friction between

Delia and Sykes. Human v. society may apply to societal assumptions about marriage and loyalty that keep Delia in this marriage. Human v. nature applies to Sykes's run-in with the snake that destroys him. And human v. himself applies to Sykes's arrogance which tells him he can control the snake that destroys him.

*Significant Quotations.*

a. The student should discuss the reference to the title. Delia is the only worker in the family and it is her "sweat" that has built their home which she is not about to leave.

b. The student should discuss Delia's loyalty in the face of abuse. Written in a time before abuse was named and socially addressed, Delia's fate is to stay with Sykes. Sykes, on the other hand, not only does no work and is physically abusive, but he also adds insult to Delia by flaunting Bertha, his girlfriend.

c. Crucial to understanding, the student should explain that this is Sykes bringing home the snake that will eventually destroy him. Sykes arrogantly claims he can handle it and brings it home to drive Delia away, while Delia is terrified of it and wants it out of the house. The snake stays in a box in the house.

d. This is the moment when Delia discovers that the snake is out of its box. The student should explain that Delia goes about doing her work only to be startled by the snake. She escapes to the barn and out of the house.

e. The student should explain that Sykes has returned home while Delia is sleeping in the hay barn. He is unaware that the snake is loose and the snake bites him. Delia hears him calling for help, but "her legs were gone flabby" and she moves toward him only after it is too late and he is swollen from the bite.

*Irony.* The irony is that Sykes brings a rattler home to destroy Delia's peace of mind and, in the end, the snake destroys the arrogant Sykes.

**Follow-up Questions. 10 Short Questions**
*These are intended for objective assessment and focus on comprehension only, purposely avoiding literary controversy.*

1. a  Indicating understanding, Delia is the worker and her labor is the reason for the very title.

2. c  We are clearly told he is with Bertha, which is a further indignation to Delia.

3. b   We are clearly told he has beaten Delia before.

4. b   Joe Clarks's porch represents the town and the clear opinion is Sykes is no good.

5. b   Crucial to understanding the crescendo of tension, Delia is very much afraid of the snake; that is why Sykes brings it home.

6. a   Also crucial, he clearly states—even brags—that he can handle the snake he has brought home.

7. c   The student can imply from the snake, the threats, and the visit to the house with Bertha when Delia is away that Sykes wants Delia out.

8. a   Delia clearly states she is not leaving. Her continual returns with the snake in the house, the one thing to scare her out, further imply that she is not leaving.

9. c   Delia remains still and only returns to Sykes when it is too late. She listens to the rattler throwing its sounds but she does not help.

10. b   Sykes is bitten in the head and is already badly swollen. "Orlando with its doctors was too far. [...] [and] she knew the cold river creeping up and up to extinguish that eye [...]." indicate that Sykes will die.

## Follow-up Questions. 5 Significant Quotations

*These are highly focused and are intended for short answer subjective assessment of comprehension only, purposely avoiding literary controversy.*

1. The student should explain the relevance to the title and that Delia is the worker, the provider for the family. Sykes, on the other hand, does nothing.

2. The student should explain that this is Delia predicting Sykes's problems to come. He has been an abuser and will die from his attempt at mentally abusing Delia with a rattlesnake.

3. The student should explain that this is the moment that Sykes brings the rattlesnake home in an attempt to make Delia miserable.

4. The student should explain the irony in this statement. Sykes arrogantly feels he can handle the rattler that he has brought to destroy Delia when, in fact, he cannot handle it at all and it will ultimately destroy him.

5. The student should explain that Sykes has been bitten and that Delia simply cannot move to help him. By the time she does move, it is too late to help this man who has abused her for years.

**Follow-up Questions. 2 Comprehension Essay Questions**

*These are highly focused and are intended for subjective assessment of comprehension only, purposely avoiding literary controversy or ancillary opinions. Intended to draw upon all facets of the story, 1 and 2 may repeat and/or complement each other.*

1. Focusing on the events of the story, the student should relate the events in logical order and note the irony therein.

2. Answers will vary greatly. The student may discuss characterization, irony, and/or events in the answer.

**Discussion Questions**

*Unlike the Follow-up Questions which are intended to measure comprehension only, thereby avoiding personal opinions and/or literary controversy, these questions are intended to elicit opinions and/or debate. Answers here are only suggestions as the literary discussion may take many forms.*

1. This asks the students to focus on the events and to reflect on their own reactions to them. There may be very heated discussion here, based on the students' own backgrounds and ethical considerations.

2. This asks the students to focus on Delia and on her survivorship. Hurston's females tend to be resilient survivors, and Delia is no exception here. Small and wiry, she does and will go on. Students should be able to draw details from the story—her work ethic, the home she supports, and so forth—that are all elements in her determination and her survival.

# CHAPTER FIVE

## *EXTENDED SHORT STORY STUDY*

# "DR. HEIDEGGER'S EXPERIMENT"

Known for raising questions, here Hawthorne seems to both question and answer the old adages, "Youth is wasted on the young," "You can't change a leopard's spots," and even "The more things [and/or people] change, the more they stay the same." He does so with dry humor and even light sarcasm in this story that is highly accessible to even the less advanced reader. This story serves as a lively introduction to Hawthorne.

**Vocabulary. Words crucial to understanding the story are presented in *Prereading Vocabulary—Context.*** However, all potentially troublesome words are listed here in the order they appear in the story, so that (1) you can easily identify words you may wish to stress and (2) you can locate them easily in the text.

# Vocabulary – "DR. HEIDEGGER'S EXPERIMENT"

1. singular
2. venerable
3. study
4. colonel
5. withered
6. melancholy
7. vigor
8. prosperous
9. merchant
10. frantic
11. speculation
12. mendicant
13. pursuit
14. brood
15. gout
16. torments
17. ruined
18. politician
19. generation
20. obscure
21. infamous
22. seclusion
23. scandalous
24. prejudiced
25. gentry
26. frequently
27. recollections
28. desirous
29. experiment
30. amuse
31. festooned
32. besprinkled
33. antique
34. folio
35. duodecimos
36. bronze
37. bust
38. accustomed
39. consultations
40. tarnished
41. gilt
42. fabled
43. deceased
44. verge
45. thitherward
46. ornamented
47. arrayed
48. faded
49. magnificence
50. brocade
51. visage
52. disorder
53. prescription
54. curiosity
55. ponderous
56. volume
57. massive
58. magic
59. chambermaid
60. ghastly
61. brazen
62. ebony
63. sustaining
64. elaborate
65. damask
66. champagne
67. exceedingly
68. eccentricity
69. nucleus
70. fantastic
71. veracious
72. stigma
73. monger
74. anticipated
75. examination
76. microscope
77. intimates
78. affirmed
79. crimson
80. hue
81. crumble
82. blossomed
83. portrait
84. peevish
85. imbibe
86. deception
87. conjurer
88. peninsula
89. gigantic
90. magnolia
91. virtue
92. acquaintance
93. fluid
94. impregnated
95. effervescent
96. ascending
97. diffused
98. cordial
99. sceptics
100. rejuvenescent
101. besought
102. peril
103. peculiar
104. feeble
105. tremulous
106. repentance
107. palsied
108. imputed
109. bestowed
110. dotage
111. decrepit

112. sapless
113. suffusion
114. inscriptions
115. patience
116. philosophic
117. delusion
118. draught
119. wrought
120. prime
121. compliments
122. sober
123. intoxicating
124. exhilaration
125. rattled
126. patriotism
127. conscience
128. deferential
129. royal ear
130. trolling
131. intermingled
132. courtesying
133. simpering
134. vanished
135. compliance
136. glitter
137. diamonds
138. dignity
139. disputed
140. quaff
141. awe
142. miserable
143. exulting
144. extremity
145. characteristic
146. mutually
147. assimilated
148. frolic

149. mock
150. decrepitude
151. astride
152. imitate
153. mirthfully
154. mischievous
155. rheumatic
156. clustered
157. chiding
158. embrace
159. rivalship
160. bewitching
161. reflected
162. contending
163. shriveled
164. coquetry
165. grappled
166. struggled
167. dashed
168. precious
169. protest
170. vale
171. exertions
172. wearied
173. ejaculated
174. fragile
175. shivered
176. furrow
177. dolefully
178. delirium
179. clasped
180. lavished
181. bemoan
182. pilgrimage

# Journal Answers

*MLA Works Cited.*

Hawthorne, Nathaniel. "Dr. Heidegger's Experiment." <u>American 24-Karat Gold</u>. 2nd ed. Ed. Yvonne Sisko. New York: Longman, 2007. 361–369.

*Main Character(s).* Dr. Heidegger, the title character, is certainly central as he initiates and orchestrates the action. Although they do not actually create the experiment, Mr. Medbourne, Colonel Killigrew, Mr. Gascoigne, and the Widow Wycherly may also be considered main characters as they are the participants in the experiment and are the very action of the story.

*Supporting Characters.* If the student has not already mentioned the four guests in *Main Characters*, the four guests most certainly must be mentioned here. They are fundamental to the experiment. The student may also mention Dr. Heidegger's deceased fiancée, whose dried rose initiates the magic. The student may also mention the water which is certainly central to the action.

*Setting.* Setting brings us, in this rather light tale, to Hawthorne's gothic trappings. In addition to the dark and somber room, the skeleton, and the medical appointments, props such as the magical mirror that reflects irreality, the magical black tome, the withered rose that returns to life, and the water service are all essential to both the atmosphere and the action. The youth-giving water arguably takes on the traits of a character and certainly is central to the action. No matter where the student might choose to change this setting, any new setting would have to be a place that would accommodate magic, for magic is essential for the story to be believable.

*Sequence. Here is an informal outline, but answers will vary.*

I. Dr. Heidegger's Guests.
   A. Mr. Medbourne is a merchant who was once wealthy, but has since lost his wealth.
   B. Colonel Killigrew is now a decaying old man who was once a ladies' man in his frivolous youth.
   C. Mr. Gascoigne is a now unknown but was once a notorious and unprincipled politician.
   D. The Widow Wycherly is now a shriveled old woman who was once a young woman of loose morals.

II. Dr. Heidegger's Experiment.
   A. Dr. Heidegger produces the dried rose from his intended wedding day and brings it back to life in water from the Fountain of Youth.

B. The four guests sample the water and return to middle age.

C. With more gulps, they become young and revert to their old characteristics, madly pursuing the Widow and ending up in confrontations.

D. In their jostling, they knock over the water and it is gone.

III. Results of the Experiment.

A. Dr. Heidegger observes that the guests have learned no wisdom in their old age, and that they have merely reverted to the same poor practices that once ruined their young lives.

B. The guests, now returned to old age without the water, all set out to find the Fountain of Youth so that they can, presumably, remain young and undisciplined forever.

*Plot. With a three-sentence limit, answers will vary.*

A doctor treats elderly friends to a return to their youth, assuming they will have learned from their past errors, but the friends all revert to their past characters and demonstrate they have learned nothing.

*Conflicts.* Human v. the supernatural is, of course, central here as the water is from the mythical Fountain of Youth and is dependent on magic. Human v. human is relevant in the confrontations that occur while pursuing the Widow. Human v. society is relevant in demonstrating the shortcomings of each of the guests, all of whom were in some way socially undesirable.

*Significant Quotations.*

a. This sets the stage for the magic as Dr. Heidegger brings out the withered rose which will return to life. The student should discuss the dark and mysterious study, the fiancée's mysterious death, and the various props which include this magical book, this rejuvenated rose, and the magical mirror that reflects dead patients, the guests in their youth and in their dotage, etc.

b. This sets the stage for the action. The student should explain the experiment wherein four elderly people will return to their youth and will demonstrate that they are still the same undisciplined people they were in their youth.

c. The student should discuss the rejuvenation of the rose, saved from the doctor's wedding suit lapel. The student might discuss the fiancée's untimely and suspicious death. The student should discuss the rose, retrieved from the magic book, that returns to life when placed in the water. This becomes demonstration and incentive for the guests to try the water.

d. The student should discuss the guests' behaviors. They cavort and caper and flirt and, ultimately, spill the magical water. Rather than returning to youth accompanied by the wisdom of the aged, they return to youth and repeat their same poor behaviors.

e. The student should reflect on the guests' behaviors. They not only return to their own, poor behaviors in youth but, once the water is spilled and they are returned to old age, they set off to find the Fountain of Youth. In contrast, the doctor disapproves of their untempered behavior and resolves the magical water is of no use if of poor use.

*Irony.* The student should comment on the central irony and related sarcasm here. People do not change and, given the chance to do better, still repeat the same misbehavior.

## Follow-up Questions. 10 Short Questions
*These are intended for objective assessment and focus on comprehension only, purposely avoiding literary controversy.*

1. b    Although the doctor philosophically questions wisdom and although the doctor seems to try to educate his guests, the skeleton and the continual references to his patients clearly make him a medical doctor.

2. c    This is clear in the text. This further tests the context vocabulary word, "mendicant." He was once a success, but his poor practices have led to his downfall.

3. c    Again, this is clear in the text. In fact, his past practices have led to his poor health in old age. Even if the student is not aware of the implied implications of "gout," it is clear that the Colonel has not been a man of virtue or of the cloth.

4. b    Again, this is clear in the text. Noted as "a man of evil fame," the story tells the student that all that is left of Mr. Gascoigne's name is the ignominy of obscurity rather than infamy.

5. c    Again, this is clear in the text. She is described as having lived in "seclusion" due to "scandalous stories" about her.

6. a    The mirror is said to reflect past, dead patients. Here it reflects the elderly in their youth and in their dotage. It is, indeed, a magical and gothic element.

7. a    Again, the water, clearly said to be from the Fountain of Youth, has the magical power to take the elderly guests back to youth. Understanding this is central to the story.

8. c   Posing this question requires close reading from the student. Yes, the rose is kept in the book and, yes, it is a reminder of the fiancée. The only correct answer here is "c," for the rose does become fresh again, but the rejuvenation is only temporary; by the end of the story, the rose is again withered.

9. a   The only correct answer is that they do become young. They do not become young forever, but rather, with the loss of the water, they revert to old age. And they certainly do not become wiser as they repeat the errors of their youth, which is the point of the story.

10. b   This negative approach demands close reading on the student's part. Yes, they do act like fools again and, yes, they do set off for the Fountain of Youth. The only thing they do not do is learn from their past experiences, which, again, is the point of the story.

## Follow-up Questions. 5 Significant Quotations

*These are highly focused and are intended for short answer subjective assessment of comprehension only, purposely avoiding literary controversy.*

1. The student should discuss the guests and the thrust of the experiment. The student should note Dr. Heidegger, a medical doctor, proposes to bring youth back to Mr. Medbourne, the ruined businessman; Colonel Killigrew, the philandering and rotting old man; Mr. Gascoigne, the fallen politician; and the Widow Wycherly, the once morally loose old woman. He proposes to observe their supposedly now wise behavior by rejuvenating each with water from the Fountain of Youth.

2. The student should describe the dark and mysterious and foreboding study, with its skeleton and magical mirror. And the student should discuss the mysterious and magical book with the withered rose it contains.

3. The student should discuss the rose. The doctor was to wear it on his wedding suit, but his fiancée mysteriously died just before the wedding. He now takes this withered rose out of the magical book and rejuvenates it in the water. The student should note that this serves as the incentive for the guests to try the water.

4. The student should comment on the guests' reversion here. They are all young again, and they are all undisciplined again. Seeming to have profited little from the wisdom of their age, they revert to the poor behaviors of their youth.

5. The student should explain that the guests, having spilled the water in their frolicking and having already demonstrated that they are none the better for their years of wisdom, are now off to seek more water and, presumably, to continue their unlearned and poor behaviors.

## Follow-up Questions. 2 Comprehension Essay Questions

*These are highly focused and are intended for subjective assessment of comprehension only, purposely avoiding literary controversy or ancillary opinions. Intended to draw upon all facets of the story, 1 and 2 may repeat and/or complement each other.*

1. This asks the student to give a general overview of the story. The story is, after all, all about Dr. Heidegger's experiment to see if his four guests, with poor behavior in the past, have learned and can return to youth and act more wisely. The experiment, of course, uses the magical rejuvenating qualities of mythical water from the Fountain of Youth. The student should discuss the four guests, the mysterious wedding death and the related rejuvenated rose that inspires them, and the resultant poor behaviors of the guests, which demonstrate that they have learned nothing.

2. This asks the student to focus on the core and even the rather cynical moral of the story: People do not learn from their errors and/or people do not change. The student should describe the characteristics of each guest during her/his youth and the actions of each guest as each regains youth and repeats her/his poor behaviors. The student should conclude that, rather than learning or growing, the guests will seek to find more magical water so that they can continue their youthful and undisciplined behavior.

## Discussion Questions

*Unlike the Follow-up Questions which are intended to measure comprehension only, thereby avoiding personal opinions and/or literary controversy, these questions are intended to elicit opinions and/or debate. Answers here are only suggestions as the literary discussion may take many forms.*

1. This makes for a lively discussion. Some like one character or another for very specific reasons and are more than willing to support their decisions with events and details from the story. These are not characters that students necessarily esteem or would emulate, but rather are simply characters that they find amusing.

2. Similar to 1, this continues the lively discussion. Again, students do not hate any characters, but rather react to them as more interesting or less interesting and, again, students are more than willing to support their decisions based on events and details from the story.

## "A ROSE FOR EMILY"

Like the other stories in this chapter, this is more complex writing intended for the more advanced reader. And this *is* Faulkner. While this is a highly anthologized story, the pedagogy here is still intended for the blossoming developmental reader and not for the Short Story 302 student. While "necrophilia" is included in context vocabulary work because this concept enhances basic comprehension, incest and homosexuality are not noted as these apply to more profound analysis and these theories are not crucial for basic understanding. Decoding symbols here may also require more sophistication than the developmental student has. Thus, *Further Writing* contains a suggestion to look up analyses on symbolism, much though Faulkner denied any intentional symbols in this story. The time shifts, the allegorical levels, and the probability that students will read this in more advanced classes make this a story recommendable for the more advanced readers. I assume anyone assigning this will have a working knowledge of this story and/or Faulkner.

**Vocabulary. Words crucial to understanding the story are presented in *Prereading Vocabulary—Context.*** However, all potentially troublesome words are listed here in the order they appear in the text, so that (1) you can easily identify words you may wish to stress and (2) you can locate them easily in the text.

# Vocabulary – "A ROSE FOR EMILY"

1. funeral
2. affection
3. monument
4. curiosity
5. cupola
6. spire
7. balcony
8. select
9. garage
10. cotton gin
11. encroach
12. august
13. coquettish
14. decay
15. bemused
16. cemetery
17. anonymous
18. Confederate
19. Union
20. tradition
21. obligation
22. mayor
23. edict
24. remitted
25. dispensation
26. perpetuity
27. charity
28. generation
29. aldermen
30. tax
31. sheriff
32. convenience
33. archaic
34. calligraphy
35. deputation
36. Negro
37. sluggishly
38. motes
39. tarnished
40. gilt
41. easel
42. descending
43. vanishing
44. ebony
45. spare
46. obesity
47. bloated
48. pallid
49. hue
50. stumbling
51. halt
52. access
53. authorities
54. vanquished
55. sweetheart
56. deserted
57. temerity
58. gross
59. teeming
60. diffident
61. slunk
62. sowing
63. cellar
64. sprinkle
65. lime
66. torso
67. idol
68. locusts
69. spraddle
70. silhouette
71. vindicated
72. insanity
73. pity
74. pauper
75. despair
76. condolence
77. grief
78. ministers
79. persuade
80. dispose
81. vague
82. resemblance
83. tragic
84. serene
85. buggy
86. bay
87. livery
88. *noblesse oblige*
89. communication
90. rustling
91. craned
92. jalousies
93. recognition
94. dignity
95. reaffirm
96. imperviousness
97. arsenic
98. poison
99. temple
100. erect
101. tilted
102. glittering
103. reins
104. interfere
105. Baptist
106. Episcopal
107. divulge
108. toilet set
109. cousin
110. cabal
111. allies

112. circumvent
113. thwart
114. virulent
115. attained
116. vigorous
117. studio
118. tedious
119. niche
120. impervious
121. tranquil
122. perverse
123. doddering
124. harsh
125. rusty
126. sibilant
127. musing
128. profoundly
129. bier
130. macabre
131. courted
132. progression
133. diminishing
134. region
135. pervading
136. tomb
137. bridal
138. valance
139. delicate
140. monogram
141. obscured
142. crescent
143. mute
144. attitude
145. embrace
146. cuckold
147. inextricable
148. patient

149. indentation
150. acrid

**Journal Answers**

*MLA Works Cited.*

Faulkner, William. "A Rose for Emily." <u>American 24-Karat Gold</u>. 2nd ed. Ed. Yvonne Sisko. New York: Longman, 2007. 379–387.

*Main Character(s).* Miss Emily or Emily Grierson is the title and the central character in this study. It is her life and her actions that are the center of everyone's interest.

*Supporting Characters.* Homer Barron, the northern "day laborer" who is unacceptable for Miss Emily's aristocracy and whom Miss Emily dates and kills and keeps in her bed, is certainly supporting. Her loyal and discreet man-servant is also supporting. Her father plays a small role and is more relevant in covert incest studies, but he is also supporting at the basic level in that he keeps her isolated. The townspeople in general who seem to report this story and/or serve as a chorus are essential. Colonel Sartoris who forgives Miss Emily's taxes, Judge Stevens who protects Miss Emily from detection, and the druggist who supplies the arsenic are all supporting. The more astute reader may even note the narrator whose position varies from townperson to observer of all.

*Setting.* The story is set in Faulkner's fictional Jefferson, which the biography mentions. More relevantly, this is set in a decaying southern town. Student may note that this can be changed to any decaying southern town, although Faulkner might not agree. The time is post Civil War to post turn of the century. The student can note that it is a time when a decaying Confederate generation can live with an emerging, newer generation, and when cars are not prevalent because Miss Emily and Homer can drive in a horse-drawn buggy while garages blight the view.

*Sequence. Here is an informal outline, but answers will vary. Note: This progresses in logical time order as opposed to Faulkner's flashbacks.*

   I. Taxes.
      A. Miss Emily is excused from paying her property taxes by Colonel Sartoris.
      B. The next generation wants to collect taxes.
      C. Miss Emily does not pay taxes.

  II. Father's death.
      A. Miss Emily's father dies.
      B. The town insists that she bury him.
      C. Cousins come from out of town.

III. Homer Barron.
   A. Homer, a northern "day laborer" working construction and of question-able heritage, dates Miss Emily.
   B. Miss Emily sees the druggist to buy poison (arsenic).
   C. Homer disappears and the town assumes he has "deserted" Miss Emily.
   D. A suspicious "smell" comes from Miss Emily's house, but the town excuses it and Judge Stevens protects Miss Emily's privacy.
IV. Miss Emily's death.
   A. Miss Emily dies.
   B. The town comes to call.
   C. The man-servant disappears.
   D. The town finds Homer's "fleshless" body lying in Miss Emily's bed in a frozen "embrace" with Miss Emily's "iron-gray" hair.

*Plot. With a three-sentence limit, answers will vary.*
An isolated and unstable woman poisons a man and then secretly keeps his body in her bed.

*Conflicts.* Human v. human applies to Miss Emily's relationships with both her father who smothers her, and Homer whom she kills. Human v. society applies to the town's intrusions and voyeurism into her life, to the unpaid taxes, to the smell issue, and, of course, to the ultimate murder issue. Human v. herself applies to Miss Emily's implied and demented murder of Homer.

*Significant Quotations.*

   a. This refers to the dispensation of taxes. The student should explain that the taxes have been forgiven by Colonel Sartoris. He says that the town owes her father money and would forgive the taxes instead. The student may discuss that the intent is to save face for Miss Emily, one of the town's resident though poor aristocracy.

   b. This refers to the new town council, made up of a younger generation, that decides Miss Emily does owe taxes. Her answer is she does not pay taxes. The student may note that this demonstrates that she is holding on to the old aristocratic ways that excuse her and, in fact, place her above the laws for others.

   c. This refers to the "smell" in the house that will eventually prove to be Homer Barron's rotting body. The student should explain that, remembering the old ways, Judge Stevens is chivalrously protecting Miss Emily with, of course, no idea of the poisoning. The student should note that the town also protects Miss Emily with the excuse that it is no wonder that the house smells, because Miss Emily only has a man-servant and men do not keep things clean like a woman.

d. The student should explain that Miss Emily goes to the druggist to buy poison. The druggist recommends the arsenic and asks what she wants it for. She does not disclose. The smell and Homer's dead body indicate she wants the poison for him.

e. The student should explain that, after Miss Emily dies, the town enters her home and finds Homer's rotted body in her bed. The student should explain that she not only poisoned him, but then kept him in her bed in what is implied to have been a continuing "embrace." The student should note that the "iron-gray" hair the town finds next to him indicates that Miss Emily is in her dead lover's arms each night.

## Follow-up Questions. 10 Short Questions
*These are intended for objective assessment and focus on comprehension only, purposely avoiding literary controversy.*

1. c   She is isolated from and does not talk to the townspeople.

2. c   Central to understanding, Miss Emily is part of a past generation that does things differently from newer times. It is this *largesse* of the past that allows her to live beyond the law.

3. b   Again, central to understanding, neither Miss Emily nor the town think she is poor or equal. She is the resident aristocracy.

4. b   Reinforcing 3 and the concept of social position, Miss Emily and all consider her the resident aristocracy.

5. c   The man-servant talks to no one and exists to protect Miss Emily. The student does not need to understanding the tacit symbolism here; at the most basic level, the man-servant is the silent and loyal domestic.

6. a   Reinforcing 5, at the most basic level, the man-servant is the silent and loyal domestic.

7. b   Miss Emily denies the death and has to be coaxed to bury her father. This is a simple fact in the story. This simple fact does not require more sophisticated understanding about the latent, covert incest theory.

8. a   This is clearly stated with the allusion to her great-aunt. Further, Miss Emily's behavior is neither sane nor normal. It is her bizarre behavior that makes the story.

9. c  The poison purchase, the smell, and Homer's "fleshless" body in a permanent "embrace" in her bed with her "iron-gray" hair by him (indicating she sleeps with the body), all clearly imply that Miss Emily has poisoned Homer.

10. b  Even if the student does not know the word "grotesque," the student must know that Miss Emily's actions are neither "normal" nor "humorous." "Grotesque" is the right word and this is a good demonstration of this word for the student.

## Follow-up Questions. 5 Significant Quotations

*These are highly focused and are intended for short answer subjective assessment of comprehension only, purposely avoiding literary controversy.*

1. This refers to the general decay of Jefferson. The student should discuss the decay of the setting in terms of both place and time. Here, the rotting appearance of the town is described. Latent in this description is the decay of time with the old generation, just as the town, in rotting disrepair.

2. This refers to the tax issue. The student should describe the "dispensation" (Colonel Sartoris decides Miss Emily will pay no taxes after her father's death and invents a story about the town owing her father money in order to save face for Miss Emily, one of Jefferson's old aristocrats). The student should note that the next generation wants to collect taxes, and Miss Emily simply does not pay the taxes based on Colonel Sartoris' arrangement, much though he is long since dead. The more astute student may note the confrontation between old times and new times.

3. This refers to the "smell" that will later prove to be Homer's poisoned and rotting body. The student should discuss the town's and Judge Stevens' excuses and the probable rotting body.

4. This refers to the purchase of the poison. The student should discuss Miss Emily's purchase of the arsenic. The more astute student may note that this again demonstrates the old ways: the aristocracy can do as it pleases.

5. This is the moment when the town finds Homer's "fleshless" body in a permanent "embrace" in Miss Emily's bed. The student should summarize the poisoning. The student should note that Miss Emily has died and that the town now finds out that she has secretly kept Homer's dead body in her bed. The student should note that Miss Emily sleeps in his dead embrace as evidenced by her "iron-gray" hair found with him. The student may note how bizarre this is.

**Follow-up Questions. 2 Comprehension Essay Questions**

*These are highly focused and are intended for subjective assessment of comprehension only, purposely avoiding literary controversy or ancillary opinions. Intended to draw upon all facets of the story, 1 and 2 may repeat and/or complement each other.*

1. It is very difficult to discuss Faulkner and avoid literary controversy and/or discussion. Homer shares the most discussed relationship in the story and Miss Emily poisons him to keep him. The developmental student will probably not discuss the homosexuality theory. In Miss Emily's relationship with her father, he isolates and keeps her. The developmental student will probably not discuss the implied covert incest issues. Miss Emily's relationships with the man-servant, Colonel Sartoris, and Judge Stevens are based on protecting her and the old order. The developmental student will probably not discuss the latent symbolism here. Although Faulkner has denied any intended symbolism in this story, in a classic dialectic, if Miss Emily personifies the rotting, white, southern gentility and the loyal Black man-servant personifies the service to and protection of that gentility, then the very servitude created by that gentility will weaken and thus internally destroy the gentility. It is unlikely the developmental student will discuss this.

2. It is the townspeople's observations of Miss Emily that tell the story. They let us know her refusal to pay taxes and imply that she is above paying taxes. They let us know she purchases the poison and finally imply that she has killed Homer and kept his corpse. They let us know she denies her father's death, state her aunt is insane, and imply she is not sane. They let us know she is the town aristocracy and repeatedly imply both her gentility and her eccentricities. The student may discuss any of these issues. The more astute student may also discuss the narrator as a person of the town; the developmental student will probably not discuss the multiple vantage points of the narrator.

**Discussion Questions**

*Unlike the Follow-up Questions which are intended to measure comprehension only, thereby avoiding personal opinions and/or literary controversy, these questions are intended to elicit opinions and/or debate. Answers here are only suggestions as the literary discussion may take many forms.*

1. Students generally enjoy this story at the narrative level because, at the narrative level, it is so creepy. This focuses students on events and they seem

to relish the events in this story. Foreshadowing can be found in all the clues—the reclusion, the smell, the poison, and so forth—all leading up to Homer's corpse in her bed. This is usually quite a lively discussion with students citing one clue after another.

2. This may take a bit of prompting and/or guidance. At first infatuated with the creepiness of it all, students may need some prompting to reflect on each strange element—the overprotective father, the necrophilia, the archaic aristocrat, and so forth—and to associate these elements as not being mere entertainment but as demonstrating decay. This is usually a very eye-opening discussion as students gain insight into the bigger picture.

# "THE MASQUE OF THE RED DEATH"

Unlike "The Tell-Tale Heart" and "The Cask of Amontillado," which the student may have read earlier, here Poe enters the world of the supernatural with the spectral figure of the Red Death. Again as always in Poe, there is much vocabulary for the student to tackle. But again, as usually with Poe, the interest in the story sustains the student. This is accessible to the middle as well as more advanced reader.

**Vocabulary. Words crucial to understanding the story are presented in *Pre-reading Vocabulary—Context*.** However, all potentially troublesome words are listed here in the order they appear in the text, so that (1) you can easily identify words you may wish to stress and (2) you can locate them easily in the text.

# Vocabulary – "THE MASQUE OF THE RED DEATH"

1. devastate
2. pestilence
3. hideous
4. Avatar
5. seal
6. profuse
7. dissolution
8. scarlet
9. ban
10. seizure
11. termination
12. incident
13. dauntless
14. sagacious
15. dominion
16. summon
17. hale
18. knight
19. dame
20. court
21. seclusion
22. castellate
23. abbey
24. extensive
25. magnificent
26. eccentric
27. august
28. lofty
29. girdle (v.)
30. courtier
31. furnace
32. massy
33. weld
34. ingress
35. egress
36. impulse
37. despair
38. frenzy
39. amply
40. provision
41. defiance
42. contagion
43. folly
44. appliance
45. buffoon
46. improvisatori
47. rage
48. furious
49. abroad
50. mask
51. voluptuous
52. masquerade
53. imperial
54. suite
55. vista
56. scarce
57. impede
58. bizarre
59. dispose
60. novel
61. gothic
62. pursue
63. winding
64. prevail
65. extremity
66. vivid
67. tapestry
68. casement
69. pend
70. emanate
71. tripod
72. brazier
73. illuminate
74. multitude
75. gaudy
76. ghastly
77. countenance
78. precinct
79. gigantic
80. ebony
81. pendulum
82. monotonous
83. circuit
84. brazen
85. peculiar
86. waltzer
87. perforce
88. evolution
89. disconcert
90. chime
91. giddy
92. sedate
93. revery
94. meditation
95. echo
96. cease
97. pervade
98. assembly
99. folly
100. tremulous
101. revel
102. fiery
103. conception
104. barbaric
105. luster
106. mad
107. fete
108. grotesque
109. piquancy
110. phantasm
111. arabesque

112. limb
113. delirious
114. wanton
115. disgust
116. stalk
117. writhe
118. hue
119. anon
120. endure
121. swell
122. wane
123. ruddy
124. sable
125. appal
126. muffle
127. peal
128. solemn
129. emphatic
130. whirl
131. commence
132. cessation
133. creep
134. leisure
135. arrest
136. rumor
137. disapprobation
138. sensation
139. license
140. bounds
141. indefinite
142. decorum
143. chord
144. reckless
145. utterly
146. jest
147. wit
148. propriety

149. gaunt
150. shroud
151. habiliment
152. visage
153. corpse
154. detect
155. dabble
156. spectral
157. image
158. solemn
159. convulse
160. shudder
161. hoarse
162. blasphemous
163. mockery
164. battlement
165. robust
166. hush
167. intruder
168. deliberate
169. awe
170. mummer
171. forth
172. vast
173. impulse
174. shrank
175. ere
176. shame
177. momentary
178. cowardice
179. aloft
180. dagger
181. impetuous
182. attain
183. confront
184. gleam
185. prostrate

186. despair
187. gasp
188. cerement
189. rude
190. tenant
191. posture
192. expire

**Journal Answers**

*MLA Works Cited.*

Poe, Edgar Allan. "The Masque of the Red Death." <u>American 24-Karat Gold</u>. 2nd ed. Ed. Yvonne Sisko. New York: Longman, 2007. 398–403.

*Main Character(s).* Prince Prospero is central. He is the one who organizes his select group, sequesters his strange castle, and provides his party atmosphere, all to keep the Red Death from his door. The figure of the Red Death—variously called "the figure," "the intruder," and "the mummer"—is the title character and is central to the story. It is the Red Death that all are escaping and it is the figure of the Red Death that brings termination to all.

*Supporting Characters.* The people in the prince's realm who are dying set the stage and are tacit support. The nobles sequestered in the castle make the party and die in the end, adding collective support to the horror. The musicians supply the music and underline the obvious discomfort at the clock's chiming. The ebony clock itself becomes a sort of foreboding character. Like the clock, the disease *per se* becomes a quasi-character and initiates the prince's actions.

*Setting.* The castle, sequestered away from the disease and sporting its individually decorated rooms, is the place. The black room specifically adds foreboding. The clock is a prop in that it is inert, while it also serves as a quasi-character with its ominous chime. The time is in the past when princes and nobles had places to go and society was simplistically rich or poor. This could be changed to any sequestered place threatened by any virulent pestilence.

*Sequence. Here is an informal outline, but answers will vary.*

   I.  The Red Death.
      A.  People are dying from this plague.
      B.  Prince Prospero decides to sequester himself and his nobles away from the disease.

  II.  The castle.
      A.  The castle has seven rooms, all decorated lively and each in a different color.
      B.  The black room with red windows that give the appearance of blood is ominous.

 III.  The masquerade ball.
      A.  All party with costumes and masks.
      B.  The band stops playing when the clock strikes.

 IV.  The figure of Red Death.

A.  The figure enters the castle and the party that were supposedly insulated against the disease.
B.  The figure infects and kills the prince.
C.  The figure infects and kills all the attendees.

*Plot. With a three-sentence limit, answers will vary.*
A proud man thinks he can cheat a disease and death, but the disease wins and slays him.

*Conflicts.* Human v. the supernatural is relevant here. The prince and his nobles are overcome by the spectral figure that brings the disease. Human v. nature is relevant only in that disease is an act of nature; that it comes through a ghoul is supernatural. Human v. society may be relevant only as it applies to the prince's poor treatment of his subjects and of the injustice this implies and that the Red Death blots out.

*Significant Quotations.*

a.  The student should explain the pestilence and the many people that have died from the dread disease.
b.  This refers to both Prince Prospero and his strange castle. The student should describe the selfish prince. The student should then describe the castle that is supposedly secreted away from the disease and that has seven vibrantly decorated areas.
c.  The student should discuss the festivities going on while others are suffering. The student should note that all are in costume for this grand ball. This is important because the figure of Red Death is not noticed at first.
d.  The student should describe the eerie sounds of the clock and the ominous black room with its red windows that seem like "besprinkled" blood.
e.  This is the moment of the Red Death. The student should describe the black shrouded but "untenanted" figure. The student should explain that this figure has brought the disease and that all—the prince first and then the others—will die.

*Symbolism.* This asks the student to reach. The student may find the figure of Red Death to represent death, justice, evil, revenge, etc. The student may find the clock to represent life or death and the black room to represent death and/or hell.

**Follow-up Questions. 10 Short Questions**
*These are intended for objective assessment and focus on comprehension only, purposely avoiding literary controversy.*

1. b  It is important that the student realize that this disease is so severe and so contagious that no one wants to be near those who have it.

2. c  Central to understanding the prince, he deserts his people and leaves not only to protect himself, but also even to party as his people suffer.

3. a  Again central, the prince most certainly thinks he can escape the disease. He deserts his people, takes only his favorites with him, and sets out to a castle he has designed to keep him safe.

4. b  Related to 4, the prince and his nobles all assume they are safe.

5. c  We are clearly told the areas are separate and are given specific descriptions of each area.

6. c  This is clearly described. The black room's only light is its red windows that give the look of blood.

7. a  The clock is ominous. Each time it strikes, the band stops playing and the people are unsettled.

8. c  "Mummer" is a consistent term used for the figure of Red Death at this point, and it is significantly a masked ball, so that with all in costumes the figure's appearance is not immediately noticed.

9. a  This measures if the student has solved "untenanted" and if the student has understood that this is a ghostly figure. The figure has to have a mask on because, after the prince's death when the guests tear at the figure, there is no figure under the costume. Further, the mummer is clearly described as being "a masked figure."

10. c  They all die in the end.

## Follow-up Questions. 5 Significant Quotations

*These are highly focused and are intended for short answer subjective assessment of comprehension only, purposely avoiding literary controversy.*

1. The student should explain the severity and the extent of the disease. It is fatal, highly contagious, and is infecting the prince's realm.

2. This refers to Prince Prospero and his castle. The student should describe the selfish prince and his eerie castle. With its seven distinct rooms, the castle is intended to insulate all from the disease.

3. The student should describe the ball and should note that the costumes serve as a cover for the entrance of the figure of the Red Death.

4. The student should describe the foreboding black room and the clock. The

room is all decorated in black with red windows that give it the look of blood. The clock strikes each hour with an ominous tone that unsettles the musicians and the revelers.

5. This is the moment just after Red Death has slain the prince and just before the rest will die. The student should describe the prince's death, the vacuous figure, and the ultimate death of all.

**Follow-up Questions. 2 Comprehension Essay Questions**
*These are highly focused and are intended for subjective assessment of comprehension only, purposely avoiding literary controversy or ancillary opinions. Intended to draw upon all facets of the story, 1 and 2 may repeat and/or complement each other.*

1. This asks the student to focus on the setting as it relates to the story. The student should describe the black room with its blood-red aspect and the ominous, ebony clock. The student should relate this to the death to come.
2. This focuses the student on the events. The student should relate the prince's intentions and the events of the story in logical order.

**Discussion Questions**
*Unlike the Follow-up Questions which are intended to measure comprehension only, thereby avoiding personal opinions and/or literary controversy, these questions are intended to elicit opinions and/or debate. Answers here are only suggestions as the literary discussion may take many forms.*

1. Students may need some prompting for this discussion. Students should reflect on the characters, the events, and the consequences, so that they can identify that even wealth and power cannot protect the sheltered characters—or sheltered people in our society—from this pestilence. AIDS and HIV are obvious parallels here as are SARS and cancer and the very condition of aging itself.
2. This dark illustration depicts the grotesque elements in the story. This asks students to focus on the prince, the ghoul, and the events in the story and to reflect upon how the illustration entwines these components.

## "THE BELL-TOWER"

This selection is one of Melville's most succinct—if one can ever call Melville succinct—works. Chosen from the *Piazza Tales*, this lively story offers the student an interesting and readable introduction to Melville. This is probably the most difficult reading here and is intended to offer a true challenge to the blossoming, more advanced reader. The Biblical references are to *Judges 4* and *5* to be found in the Appendix.

**Vocabulary. Words crucial to understanding the story are presented in *Pre-reading Vocabulary—Context*.** However, all potentially troublesome words are listed here in the order they appear in the story, so that (1) you can easily identify words you may wish to stress and (2) you can locate them easily in the text.

# Vocabulary – "THE BELL-TOWER"

1. nigh
2. fresco
3. dank
4. mould
5. canker
6. plain
7. Anak
8. Titan
9. dissolution
10. mound
11. perish
12. immutable
13. gauge
14. prostration
15. steadfast
16. lichen
17. chime
18. aviary
19. foundling
20. Babel
21. renovate
22. deluge
23. submersion
24. jubilant
25. Noah
26. Shinar
27. aspiration
28. enrich
29. commerce
30. Levant
31. noble
32. repute
33. architect
34. torch
35. mason
36. ascend
37. summit
38. scheme
39. lofty
40. throng
41. rude
42. scaffolding
43. bough
44. homage
45. viol
46. ordnance
47. course
48. mount
49. erect
50. Alps
51. crest
52. invisible
53. thence
54. combustion
55. applause
56. serenity
57. perch
58. durst
59. periodic
60. correspond
61. receptacle
62. minor
63. singular
64. suspension
65. execute
66. unite
67. distinct
68. attest
69. founder
70. lavish
71. elate
72. magistrate
73. dependent
74. sway
75. mass
76. deter
77. mammoth
78. kindle
79. balsamic
80. tide
81. bay (vb.)
82. hound
83. fatal
84. dreaded
85. Shadrach
86. smote
87. culprit
88. smitten
89. splinter
90. seethe
91. Thebes
92. disinter
93. blemish
94. devise
95. scorn
96. homicide
97. charitable
98. deed
99. impute
100. esthetic
101. flagitious
102. charger
103. felony
104. remit
105. absolution
106. conscience
107. republic
108. hoist
109. pomp
110. solitude
111. ensue

112. belfry
113. insight
114. seclusion
115. mystery
116. pertain
117. forbidden
118. cloak
119. procedure
120. elaborate
121. sculpture
122. statue
123. edifice
124. expose
125. critical
126. appointed
127. statuary
128. observe
129. rigid
130. pliant
131. attain
132. obscure
133. crane
134. blacksmith
135. venture
136. suspicion
137. surmise
138. augment
139. demur
140. associate
141. elderly
142. image
143. recompense
144. plausible
145. entrench
146. concede
147. attitude
148. perplex
149. conceal

150. violent
151. muffle
152. domino
153. warp
154. woven
155. grating
156. lattice
157. perturb
158. imagination
159. discern
160. slight
161. fitful
162. incidental
163. insignificant
164. pry
165. corrode
166. encrust
167. mockery
168. brazen
169. fusion
170. merest
171. gaze
172. incognito
173. Venetian
174. vague
175. apprehension
176. lest
177. descend
178. affect
179. merriment
180. disquietude
181. relieve
182. coarse
183. canvas
184. insensible
185. hitherto
186. caster
187. trait

188. accomplish
189. precede
190. devote
191. elaborate
192. patient
193. chisel
194. latent
195. shy
196. garland
197. choral
198. embody
199. excel
200. hark
201. yonder
202. equivocal
203. forbear
204. allusion
205. plebian
206. placid
207. dignity
208. anxious
209. assure
210. stroke
211. adorn
212. sever
213. precise
214. advance
215. clasp
216. liege
217. litter
218. illustrious
219. vassal
220. Vulcan
221. forge
222. ostentatious
223. deference
224. scuttle
225. escort

226. sardonic
227. disdain
228. lurk
229. humble
230. mien
231. sympathy
232. distress
233. surmise
234. cynic
235. solitaire
236. influence
237. thereupon
238. forebode
239. impulsive
240. prophetess
241. resume
242. jocund
243. abandon
244. inquire
245. discrepancy
246. curb
247. variance
248. stake
249. heedful
250. shaft
251. leeward
252. ample
253. bar
254. duplicate
255. grave (vb.)
256. ancestor
257. impression
258. identical
259. scan
260. gravity
261. benevolent
262. ambiguous
263. scrutiny

264. incipient
265. malign
266. linear
267. suffice
268. transmute
269. mortar
270. arch
271. forbidding
272. personality
273. soul
274. bland
275. intent
276. gaze
277. consequence
278. shift
279. pardon
280. signor
281. supercilious
282. foe
283. whim
284. sod
285. chill
286. gloom
287. whence
288. emerge
289. custom
290. proclamation
291. meridian
292. accompaniment
293. encamp
294. mental
295. disturb
296. suppress
297. plaining (n.)
298. engine
299. overply
300. concourse
301. blur

302. principal
303. citizen
304. cavalcade
305. impatience
306. scrutinize
307. verge
308. expectation
309. Shiloh
310. pervade
311. swarming
312. mangle
313. naught
314. audible
315. multitude
316. tumultuous
317. hail
318. hush
319. stationing
320. surge
321. winding
322. spectacle
323. spaniel
324. brake
325. snuff
326. prostrate
327. coincide
328. vertical
329. impend
330. limb
331. clad
332. scaly
333. mail
334. lustrous
335. manacle
336. clubbed
337. smite
338. insert
339. spurn

340. immediate
341. involuntary
342. doubt
343. horrify
344. arquebus
345. report
346. fierce
347. whiz
348. din
349. dash
350. pavement
351. wreath
352. aver
353. slight
354. burial
355. circumstance
356. instinctive
357. panic
358. smuggle
359. urgency
360. convivial
361. twain
362. supernatural
363. agency
364. inference
365. absent
366. defective
367. tradition
368. explicit
369. preserve
370. dearth
371. requisite
372. supposition
373. entertain
374. motive
375. mode
376. origin
377. assume

378. penetrate
379. peculiar
380. agitation
381. percussion
382. cumbrous
383. stalwart
384. sentry
385. shelter
386. opine
387. derive
388. scheme
389. mast
390. spire
391. reduction
392. obliterate
393. intelligent
394. feature
395. evince
396. volition
397. gesture
398. resemble
399. automatic
400. telegraph
401. aspect
402. behold
403. vital
404. sally
405. locomotion
406. conjecture
407. acquaintance
408. enterprising
409. intimate
410. prompted
411. subtle
412. substitute
413. seldom
414. insensible
415. gradation

416. pigmy
417. eventuality
418. daring
419. partial
420. ulterior
421. Helot
422. universal
423. convenience
424. supplement
425. serf
426. cunning
427. fiery
428. serpent
429. chimera
430. contrary
431. marvelous
432. apparently
433. transcend
434. bound
435. divine
436. creation
437. propose
438. sober
439. affirm
440. skeptic
441. scorn
442. metaphysic
443. germ
444. correspondence
445. partake
446. philosopher
447. physiological
448. chemical
449. induction
450. qualify
451. manufacture
452. improve
453. aught

454. alchemist
455. species
456. incantation
457. evoke
458. vitality
459. sanguine
460. theosophist
461. vouchsafe
462. materialist
463. crucible
464. conjure
465. altar
466. intrigue
467. stoop
468. theurgy
469. heroic
470. initial
471. fanciful
472. utilitarian
473. ambition
474. collaterally
475. organism
476. supposition
477. threshold
478. catastrophe
479. retreat
480. groove
481. junction
482. retire
483. bide
484. axis
485. mace
486. perish
487. resonance
488. cling
489. intervene
490. infallible
491. deft

492. intensify
493. absorb
494. abate
495. oblivious
496. dull
497. hover
498. poise
499. clog
500. chisel
501. genius
502. stately
503. jeopardize
504. timidity
505. bier
506. cathedral
507. robust
508. pall-bearer
509. naught
510. groin (vb.)
511. concentrate
512. quake
513. ponderous
514. sward
515. invert
516. disinterment
517. fracture
518. defect
519. deceptive
520. minute (adj.)
521. subsequent
522. molten

## Journal Answers

*MLA Works Cited.*

Melville, Herman. "The Bell-Tower." <u>American 24-Karat Gold</u>. 2nd ed. Ed. Yvonne Sisko. New York: Longman, 2007. 414–426.

*Main Character(s).* Bannadonna is certainly the central character. He is the architect and artisan who is commissioned to create the bell-tower. His creation and his *hubris* are the core of the story. The student may also list Haman, Bannadonna's creation, here. Haman is the human/robot who slays Bannadonna.

*Supporting Characters.* If the student has not already listed Haman, he should be listed here. The magistrates who check up on Bannadonna are also supporting and help to build the tension. The town itself is supporting as it commissions and then awaits the bell-tower's completion. Bannadonna's workmen are also supporting. Especially relevant is the worker whom Bannadonna "smote" and who dies a fiery death inside the bell casting, leaving a "blemish" that ultimately destroys the bell creation.

*Setting.* This is set in Renaissance Italy. Anywhere and any time a town might commission a magnificent structure can be used.

*Sequence. Here is an informal outline, but answers will vary. Note: This progresses in logical time order.*

I. The tower and the bell.
   A. The tower is built.
   B. The bell is cast.
      1. Bannadonna designs a tremendous structure.
      2. A worker gets in his way and, after Bannadonna strikes the worker, the worker falls into the metal mix and causes a blemish.
      3. Bannadonna is cleared of any charges in the murder.

II. Sculpting.
   A. Bannadonna sculpts twelve women's/hour's faces into the bell, to be struck and cause a different sound each hour.
   B. The first hour, Una, resembles the Biblical prophetess Deborah.
   C. Bannadonna creates Haman, the human/robot ringer who will slay Bannadonna.

III. Bell to ring at one.
   A. The town gathers for the first unveiling.
   B. All hear a ghastly noise, but no bell.
   C. The magistrates ascend the tower and find Bannadonna dead at the hand of Haman.

D. Haman is dismounted and dropped far out at sea.

IV. Reasons.

A. In a classic dialectic, Bannadonna created his own doom in Haman.

B. In a demonstration of *hubris,* Bannadonna tried to create some being better than that produced by nature and by God.

V. The end.

A. At Bannadonna's funeral, the bell crashes to the ground.

B. The blemish—of the dead worker—is found in the bell.

C. On the tower's first anniversary, the entire tower crashes to the ground, never to be rebuilt.

*Plot. With a three-sentence limit, answers will vary.*

A proud man decides to create a tower with a mechanical man that is better than man created by God, and the mechanical creation ultimately kills the proud man.

*Conflicts.* Man v. machine is relevant in Bannadonna's death by Haman. Man v. the supernatural is also relevant in Bannadonna's death by Haman. Man v. society is relevant in the murder Bannadonna is forgiven and in the magistrates' suspicions. And man v. himself is relevant in the dialectic Bannadonna self-creates by letting his *hubris* lead him to build a creature that is better than that created by nature or God.

*Significant Quotations.*

a. The student should describe Bannadonna as an exceptional and recognized architect and metal worker. The student might also note Bannadonna's high esteem of himself.

b. The student should describe the bell-tower that is now constructed and the clock-tower that is now awaiting Bannadonna's invention.

c. The student should discuss the bell casting and the death of the worker. The bell is tremendous and, in anger, Bannadonna "smote" a worker who ends up melted in the bell. The worker's remains, however, leave a blemish and this will later prove the weakness in the bell. The student should also note that Bannadonna is cleared of the "felony" and/or murder.

d. The student should describe Haman, Bannadonna's superhuman super-machine.

e. The student should explain the demise of Bannadonna, who is slain by his invention. The student should be able to explain Sisera from the Biblical references provided in the Appendix.

*Symbolism. Answers will vary.*

The student may find Haman symbolizing pride, over-perfection, and self-destruction.

## Follow-up Questions. 10 Short Questions

*These are intended for objective assessment and focus on comprehension only, purposely avoiding literary controversy.*

1. b  Bannadonna is clearly referred to as the best in Europe at the time.

2. a  He seems most comfortable in his tower—the magistrate even comments on this—and even tries to keep others out to leave him alone.

3. c  This refers to the incident when Bannadonna hits the worker who falls into the bell metals and is killed, leaving a fatal blemish in the bell.

4. b  Bannadonna clearly tells us that the twelve women, or hours, will result in each hour sounding differently.

5. a  It is central to understanding that Haman, the robot ringer, seems to be human.

6. c  The magistrate describes Una's face as looking like Deborah, predicting doom.

7. a  The young magistrate is very curious about Haman. Bannadonna, in response, ushers both magistrates down from the tower.

8. a  Although Haman is male and Jael is female, in the Biblical reference Una is the prophetess Deborah, Bannadonna is the slain Sisera, and Haman is Jael the slayer.

9. c  One reason given for Haman's actions is that the oil can spilled too much. The reason, of course, is Haman's supernatural power.

10. b  Haman, the creation, slays Bannadonna, the creator.

## Follow-up Questions. 5 Significant Quotations

*These are highly focused and are intended for short answer subjective assessment of comprehension only, purposely avoiding literary controversy.*

1. The student should discuss the erection of the bell-tower and the overly ambitious bell that Bannadonna has designed. It will be the bell's ringing structure that ultimately destroys Bannadonna.

2. The student should discuss the death of the worker. In anger, Bannadonna hits the worker while casting the bell and the worker falls in the metal. The worker dies, and Bannadonna is forgiven the "felony."

3. The student should discuss the death of Bannadonna.

4. The student should discuss the death of Bannadonna. With Una looking like the Biblical prophetess Deborah, Bannadonna's unholy creation, Haman, kills Bannadonna.

5. The student should explain that Bannadonna's intent is to better nature and God. The student should comment that in creating Haman, Bannadonna's very pride has sealed his doom.

## Follow-up Questions. 2 Comprehension Essay Questions

*These are highly focused and are intended for subjective assessment of comprehension only, purposely avoiding literary controversy or ancillary opinions. Intended to draw upon all facets of the story, 1 and 2 may repeat and/or complement each other.*

1. This focuses the student on the events. The student should explain the construction of the tower, and the arrogant ambition in creating the bell and the human-like ringer for the clock.

2. This focuses the student on Bannadonna's self-destruction. Bannadonna sets out to create a being superior to that which nature and God have created. The student will probably have little familiarity with Greek tragedy, but this question asks the student to think in classic tragic terms.

## Discussion Questions

*Unlike the Follow-up Questions which are intended to measure comprehension only, thereby avoiding personal opinions and/or literary controversy, these questions are intended to elicit opinions and/or debate. Answers here are only suggestions as the literary discussion may take many forms.*

1. Students studying this story will already be at a rather sophisticated level. Here students must reflect on Bannadonna, on Haman, on the statues, on the events in the story, and on the Biblical references that demonstrate and even predict Bannadonna's demise. Bannadonna sets out to create better than God and is struck down for this.

2. "The Bell-Tower" is a perfect if diabolical demonstration of this dialectic dynamic. Bannadonna (the thesis) creates Haman (the antithesis) and the antithesis destroys the thesis (the synthesis). Students may need some prompting, but focusing on the events in the story should fuel this rich discussion.

# INDEX OF AUTHORS AND TITLES

# NOTES